Everyday Evangelism

Witnessing
That
Works

by Ray Comfort

Huntington House Publishers

Huntington House Publishers
P.O. Box 53788
Lafayette, Louisiana 70505

Library of Congress Card Catalog Number
95-75885
ISBN 1-56384-091-X

Printed in the U.S.A.

Unless otherwise indicated, all Scripture
quotations are taken from the *King James*
and the *New King James* version of the Bible.

Dedication

To my good friends
and fellow laborers in the gospel:
Brennan Hartley, Randy Jones, Dan Jarvis,
Jeff Chapman, Mike Smalley, Patrick Essian,
Lloyd Craycroft, Hans Frist, Harry Brut,
Howard Jones, Paul & Mary Jorgensen, Grant
Berry, Erik Hollander, Jamie Donaldson,
Barry & Amie Howard and Steven Smith.

Contents

Foreword   vii

Chapter 1   9
  The Lips of the Righteous

Chapter 2   23
  God's Ways Are Our Ways

Chapter 3   33
  I Know a Diamond When I See One!

Chapter 4   45
  The Doctor with No B.A.

Chapter 5   69
  Running on Water

Chapter 6   81
  Too Much at Steak

Chapter 7   93
        Mine Eyes Have Seen the Glory

Chapter 8   107
        Necessity Is Laid Upon Me

Chapter 9   119
        Fired For Succeeding

Chapter 10   141
        Stirred to a Frenzy

Chapter 11   165
        We Are Not Ignorant of His Devices

Chapter 12   183
        A Well-trained Housemaid

Foreword

Ray's book is a gauntlet thrown on the ground to a man-centered gospel that puts human need above divine right, preaches happiness without holiness and offers a fire escape without ever daring to mention the fire.

We will lose a whole generation if we do not speak the truth in love. Woe unto us if we do not preach the gospel!

That grand old giant of spiritual warfare, William Booth of the Salvation Army, once prophesied of the coming twentieth century. He warned of a generation to come that preached a faith without repentance, religion without the Holy Spirit, a salvation without Lordship and a Christianity without Christ. That generation has come, and Ray Comfort has declared war. This time demands spiritual soldiers. That's what this book is all about.

—Winkie Pratney

ONE

The Lips of the Righteous

In 1967, before my conversion, I worked in a bank. Each morning, it was my task to deliver checks from one bank to another. One day, I noticed a crowd of about 150 people packed around the entrance of a department store. The store was having a massive sale, and as a draw card, they had some incredible bargains displayed in the window. One of the reduced items was a jacket, with a giveaway price tag of only two dollars. As far as I was concerned that jacket was made for Comfort. I wanted it, but there was no way I could get it with so many people waiting at the entrance of the store.

After my deliveries, I made my way back to the store. I waited until about twenty seconds before 9:00 A.M., stood at the back of the crowd and said with a loud, authoritative voice, "Excuse me!" People at the back looked around, saw my black briefcase, and concluded the obvious. This was the man whose job it was to open the door and let everyone into the store.

It was in their interest to get me to the front of
the crowd as quickly as possible.

As I said, "Excuse me . . . stand back please,
excuse me," people began saying, "Let him
through please," and they opened up like the
Red Sea. The timing was perfect. When I approached the door, a gentleman on the other
side turned a key, and suddenly the dam of
human bodies burst, pushing me into the store
and straight to the goal of my jacket, which I
purchased for two dollars.

How much do you want to break out of
your comfort zone and live on the cutting edge
of God's will? If you desire it above all else,
then set your sights on it, and don't let anything
deter you from that goal. Set your face "as a
flint towards Jerusalem." You have a large crowd
to push through, and some won't move out of
the way as quickly as others. Self-will will be
your biggest obstacle. He will take some prod-
ding with your case. Directly behind him is his
best friend, the ever satisfied and overweight
Self-indulgence. He is more interested in eating
a donut than he is in moving out of your way.
Just beside him is Laziness, and his two bedfel-
lows, Apathy and Hard-heart. Pride will stand
arrogantly in front of you and will persist in
keeping his position. He will be wearing the
disguise of the "fear of man," so he may be
hard to recognize.

Condemnation, Doubt and Discouragement
will whisper lies in your ear to try and take your
eyes off your goal. They can be dealt with

through faith in God's promises. Watch them though, because they will be wanting to move back the moment you push them aside.

Then you have to maneuver passed the attractive subtleties of Legitimate Pleasure, Entertainment and Leisure. They will want you to stop and talk for a while.

The fundamental principle to getting each hindrance to move back is the authority you and I have in Christ. What I did to get that jacket was deceitful. I let those people think that I was something I wasn't. But, if you are in Christ, you are a son or daughter of the most High God. The flesh, with all its appetites, is no longer a puppet for the devil. The strings were cut at Calvary. Jesus Christ gave you the right to boldly approach the throne of grace. God will open doors at just the right time for you to get your heart's desire.

It is your blood-bought right to break out of the comfort zone of mediocrity, obscurity, mundane and defeatist Christianity, and live on the cutting edge of the will of the Living God. Let's look at how you can do that.

Whose Idea Was It?

A young man sat in my office with a very troubled expression on his face. He had been seeking God's will for his life and had come to a point of total frustration. He didn't know what on earth God wanted him to do. So, I shared a simple key to unlocking the will of God, something which had been a guiding principle by which I lived since I was converted at the age of twenty-two. I had been apprehensive to share the key with anyone, but the young man so appreciated what I told him, I decided to begin teaching it from the pulpit, and to my surprise, it was also appreciated in the pew.

I reminded him of the incident where David slew Goliath, and asked him whose idea it was for the youth to fight the giant. He thought for a moment, and then said, "David's." He was right. If you take the time to study 1 Samuel chapter 17, you will see that there is no record of him seeking God for His will in this instance. How could this be? The Scriptures say, "Acknowledge Him in all your ways and He will direct your paths." Shouldn't David have acknowledged the Lord in some way? No doubt, he did pray as he faced his enemy, but there is no record of David asking God whether or not he should attack the giant Philistine.

The reason for this is clear. The Bible tells us in Proverbs 10:32, "The lips of the righteous know what is acceptable." There are certain things in life that we know are not acceptable. If you saw an elderly lady fall to the ground, do you ask God whether or not you should help her up? Certain things should be obvious to the godly. David took one look at the situation and saw that such a thing was completely unacceptable—that this "uncircumcised Philistine" should defy the armies of the Living God.

David could draw that conclusion because he had a relationship with God. His senses were "exercised to discern both good and evil." He knew the Lord, and "they that know their God shall do exploits."

Doing Your Own Thing

The thought that may come to mind, is that the Christian must be careful not to move into the area of what is commonly called "presumption." There is an incident in Scripture where Israel presumed God was with them when He wasn't, and the result was great tragedy. However, the issue is clarified the moment one understands the difference between faith and presumption. Take for instance my faith in my wife. Sue loves me and takes care of me. She keeps the house clean and tidy to a point where I am proud to have visitors. I have great faith in her. But presumption says, "You guys leave that mess there, the wife will clean it up . . . best housemaid I ever had!" The dictionary defines the word presumption as "an arrogant taking for granted, a liberty."

Love, respect and faith go hand in hand, and I trust that I never presume upon my wife. In the same way, each of us should love and fear God enough never to have an arrogant attitude of taking Him for granted. In fact, he who knows and fears his God would never take Him for granted—he will not venture into presumption. Yet, so many are so afraid of presumption they won't step out in faith. They are so scared of "doing their own thing," that they don't do anything for God.

It is interesting to note that the Apostle Paul rejoiced even when certain professing Christians "did their own thing" when preaching the gospel. Look at his words:

> Some, indeed, preach Christ out of contention, not sincerely, supposing to add affliction to my bonds; but the other, of love, knowing that I am set for the defense of the Gospel. What then? Notwithstanding, every way whether in pretence or in truth, Christ is preached; and in that I do rejoice, yea, and will rejoice. (Phil. 1:15-18)

For many years, I crossed swords with a man called the Wizard. The man was a very eloquent speaker who would dress up in all sorts of costumes to attract large crowds. His message varied from things of interest to stupidity. He would provoke thought by saying how senseless it is that we pay doctors when we are sick. It is not in the interest of the medical profession for you to be healthy. If we are in good health, our doctors have no income, so there's no great incentive for them to work for our well-being. It would be far more sensible for us to pay our doctors five dollars for every month we are well. Then they would have a reason to keep us in health.

We were both open-air speakers and had a mutual understanding that I preached to the first lunch hour crowds in the local square, and he preached to the second. This happened almost daily for twelve years. Some days he would arrive while I was still speaking, and would sud-

denly burst from the crowd and verbally tear
into me. I loved it. In fact, he was my best
heckler. People thought I had great courage,
but I knew that afterwards we would go off
together for a cup of tea. The Wizard and myself were what I called, "friendly enemies."

This man was very anti-Christian. He would,
much to the delight of the public, make an altar
to the God of Israel and sacrifice a ten-dollar
bill by fire to God, in the name of the Father,
the Son and the Holy Spirit. I was always surprised at God's patience with him. On a scale of
evil, the Wizard was seven out of ten.

I also had another regular heckler whose
name was Bernard. On a scale of ten, Bernard
was on twenty seven. He would say and do things
in public that would make your hair curl. He
was so anti-Christian, he made Saul of Tarsus
seem like Mary Poppins. With cutting sarcasm
and a blazing contempt, he would say things
like, "Jesus died for your sins. You have to repent because God has appointed a Day in which
He will judge the world in righteousness." One
day he was spitting out hatred with such intensity, he embarrassed himself by accidentally
spitting out his false teeth. I almost choked with
joy.

What should our attitude be to such a man?
We should grieve that he was so anti-Christian,
but our grief should be for him, not for God—
"Be not deceived, God is not mocked. Whatever a man sows, that will he also reap." It didn't
worry me at all when he repeated Scripture,

because like Paul, I rejoice, even when Christ is preached from such an evil motive. The reason for this is that the quality is in the seed, not in the sower. A farmer can, with great proficiency, place his skillful hands in the sack of seed and scatter it on the soil. It will produce fruit if it falls on good soil. A simpleton can place his unskilled hands in the same sack and scatter the same seed, and it will also produce fruit, because the quality is in the seed and not in the sower. This is of great consolation to me. I know that God doesn't require my ability, just my availability to take the quality seed of His Word and scatter it on the soil of men's hearts.

Let me give you an example of this principle. Around the time Bernard was evilizing, a young man approached me and said, "I have been listening to the gospel for some time, and I gave my life to Christ last Monday." I said how pleased I was and asked him for details. The young man heard Bernard spewing out blasphemies in his usual anti-Christian, mocking fashion. After listening to him for some time, the man was so disgusted, he went somewhere quiet and gave his life to Jesus. The quality was in the seed of God's Word, and it found a place in his heart even when it was thrown down in ridicule.

Paul rejoiced that somebody, even out of a wrong motive, was scattering the seed of the Word of God, because anybody scattering the seed is better than nobody scattering seed. With these consoling thoughts in mind, to illustrate another important principle, I now want to share with you four small exploits that God allowed me to be involved in.

A few months after my conversion in 1972, I suddenly felt inspired to buy a bus to use for evangelism. This sudden flash of thought came when I was driving through Aranui, a suburb of my hometown. I placed an advertisement in the church column of a local newspaper to purchase a bus, and when nothing came of it, I put the idea aside.

Two or three months later, I was driving through that same portion of Aranui, when I felt impressed to pray again for a bus. I could see it in my mind's eye. I would have Scripture painted in quality sign-writing all around the bus. I would take out the seats and rearrange them around the walls, and lay plush carpet on the floor. It could be used for counseling, for prayer, and for transporting Christians to preach the gospel. When I arrived home, a friend called and read me a verse from the Book of Acts about turning "those who are in darkness to light." That night at a prayer meeting, another friend stuffed two hundred dollars into my pocket (I liked that guy). The next day, God confirmed His Word with the kind of signs most of us enjoy, by supplying finances from four different directions. It was about that time that I heard of a bus auction and went to it with faith, a friend and finances.

As I waited for the first bus to be auctioned, I had a sense of anticipation as to what the

Lord was going to do. It was just a matter of waiting and clutching onto my grand total of six hundred dollars. Unfortunately, the first of the three buses to be auctioned went for $1,790. I felt devastated, so I went for a long walk. It was then that God spoke to my heart with the words, "Lean not to your own understanding." The second bus sold for fourteen hundred, still well above our price range. We left the auction for a quick lunch, but upon our return, found that the auctioneers had changed, this one was fast and the auction had finished. I felt the air drain out of my lungs as we leaned against our lost bus and gave God thanks anyway.

We didn't say too much on the way home. Then, while driving back through Aranui, along the portion of road where I first prayed, I noticed a large bus parked in a field. We stopped the car, and I went next door to see if I could locate the owner.

I looked through the back door and saw a middle-aged man who was fixing something on the floor at the end of a hallway. The bus belonged to him, so I asked if he was interested in selling it. He stood to his feet, scratched his head, and said, "That's really strange . . . I was just thinking of selling it."

God gave me my bus for a grand total of six hundred dollars, and it was twice the size I had envisaged. We tore out the old seats, carpeted it throughout, and put new seating around the walls. The destination on the front said "Heaven." We put Scriptures around the outside, and also painted a large picture of a man in a coffin on the back of the bus. Piled around him were masses of money and the words, "What shall it profit a man, if he gains the whole world, and loses his own soul." We didn't get too many tailgaters.

It was a big bus. In fact, it was so big, I steered the thing while Sue worked the pedals. One day I was driving through the city and found that it was so big, I couldn't get it around a corner. I carefully checked the rear view mirrors, and backed up. It was then that I heard a sound I will never forget. It was a high-pitched "Ne-ne-ne-ne-ne-ne!" with a "scrrrraaaaape" following it. I checked my mirrors again. Nothing there . . . and drove forward. Again I heard the mystifying "scrrrraaaaape" noise, so I pulled in around the corner to check what I thought was something dragging under the bus.

Suddenly, there was a feverish knock on the door. I opened it and saw a young man with a pale face. He had been parked directly behind the bus in a very small car, when a coffin with "What shall it profit a man if he gains the whole world and loses his soul," began heading towards him. He honked his car horn "Ne-ne-ne-ne-ne-ne!" as the bus scraped across the hood of his car taking the corpse, the coffin and the Scripture right up to his windshield. I think God was speaking to that man. Over the years, the bus traveled thousands of miles and was a means of taking the gospel to many.

Locked Out

The second exploit was a tabloid Jesus paper called "Living Waters." This twelve-page newspaper had no income from advertising, no subscription fee and after the first issue, we never asked for financial support. We saw God supply finances for a total of 359,000 copies which were given away. On one occasion, I had ordered literature with only $5.75 in the bank. Sometime later, we found a paper sack with over forty twenty-dollar bills in it at our front door. The Scripture which motivated us to get the bus and start the paper was solely, "Go into all the world and preach the gospel to every creature."

The third exploit was the writing of our first book. I had previously published an eight-page paper called "My Friends Are Dying," and felt that there was an opening for the gospel through a paperback with the same name. It was after I began writing the first chapter that the verse was quickened, "Commit your works unto me and I will establish your thoughts." The first edition wasn't brilliantly written, but God blessed it anyway, and it sold between fifteen and twenty thousand copies, and is now in its ninth print. The Scripture that motivated me to write the book was, "Go into all the world and preach the gospel to every creature."

Three years after the book, we felt that a movie of the same name could also be an opportunity to share the gospel, so we committed our ways to the Lord and He established our thoughts. Over a period of time, He supplied the necessary twenty-four thousand dollars to pay for the production costs. An amazing twenty-three hundred people showed up to the premiere. The theater was so packed, a thousand had to be locked out and an unscheduled second viewing held. Since that time, it has been screened hundreds of times, and seed has been sown in the hearts of many unsaved. God didn't tell me to get a bus, start a paper, write a book or make a movie—the sole motivation for those exploits was the same, "Go into all the world and preach the gospel to every creature."

TWO

God's Ways Are Our Ways

When things don't work out as we think they should, we often quote Isaiah 55:8: "For My thoughts are not your thoughts, neither are your ways My ways, says the Lord." God's ways are above our ways, and often we have no idea why He allows certain things to happen. But the Scripture we so often lean on for consolation is not directed at the godly. Here it is in context:

> Seek the Lord while He may be found, call upon Him while He is near. Let the wicked forsake his way, and the unrighteous man his thoughts. . . . For My thoughts are not your thoughts, neither are your ways My ways, says the Lord. (Isa. 55:6-8)

God is directing Himself to the wicked and the unrighteous man. He is speaking to the unregenerate, those whose "carnal mind is at enmity" with Him, who "walk in the vanity of their mind, having the understanding darkened."

23

Before we trust in the Savior, we are enemies of God in our minds through wicked works, and even our thoughts are an abomination to the Lord (Prov. 15:26). Like a lost sheep, we have also "gone astray," we have "turned every one to his own way," and our ways are an abomination to the Lord (Prov. 15:9).

Upon conversion, God puts His Law into our minds (Heb. 8:10), giving us a new mind, the "mind of Christ," and renewing us in the "spirit" of our minds. He gives us a "new and living way" (Heb. 10:20). Now God's ways are our ways and God's thoughts become our thoughts. We are led by the Spirit, walking "in His ways" (Ps. 119:3).

Once, our lives were dead in trespasses, governed by sin, selfishness, Satan, the soul and senses. But God made us alive in our spirit. Now we walk in the Spirit, have the mind of the Spirit, worship in the Spirit and live in the Spirit. If we are walking in the Spirit, with our Adamic nature crucified, we can therefore be assured that the desires we now have are in line with God's desires. For example, before I was a Christian, it never entered my mind to start a Jesus paper, or get a bus and put Bible verses all around it—it would have been the last thing I would have been interested in. Now my desires are radically different.

I'm sure few of us have failed to underline Psalm 37:4 in our Bibles: "Delight yourself in the Lord, and He shall give you the desires of

your heart." But what are our desires? What do
we want most in life? Do we desire above all
things to have a better paying job, a bigger
house, thicker carpet, a superior car and more
money? Are we controlled by the lust of the
flesh, the lust of the eyes and the pride of life,
or have we been transformed from the way of
this world by "the renewing of [our] mind," that
we may prove what is that good, and acceptable, and perfect will of God? Are our desires
now in line with God's desires? Are we above
all things "not willing that any should perish,"
that all men come to the knowledge of the truth?
If that is our testimony, it is because we have
the same Spirit in us as the Apostle Paul, who
said, "For it is God who works in me to both
will and do of His good pleasure" (Phil. 2:13).
Look at this verse in the Amplified Bible:

> Not in your own strength for it is God who
> is all the while effectually at work in you—
> energizing and creating in you the power
> and desire—both to will and to work for
> His good pleasure and satisfaction and
> delight.

Scripture tells me that the reason I get desires to do exploits for God is because He is in
me "energizing and creating in me the power
and desire to work for His pleasure." When I
get aspirations to do things to reach the unsaved,
it is because my desires have become His desires, and His desires have become my desires.
I can pursue my aspirations, trusting that they

are in the will of God, and therefore I can confidently expect Him to honor them. Remember, this is not presumption, "an arrogant taking for granted," but a pure, unadulterated desire to do the right thing by reaching out to the lost.

Let me ask you another question. Whose idea was it for Peter to walk on water? See if you can detect whose idea it was in these verses:

> Now in the fourth watch of the night Jesus went to them, walking on the sea. And when the disciples saw Him walking on the sea, they were troubled, saying, "It is a ghost!" And they cried out for fear. But immediately Jesus spoke to them, saying, "Be of good cheer! It is I; do not be afraid." And Peter answered Him and said, "Lord, if it is you, command me to come to you on the water." So He said, "Come." And when Peter had come down out of the boat, he walked on the water to go to Jesus. (Matt. 14:25-29)

Peter said, "Lord, if it is you, command me to come to you on the water." Peter had the idea, and Jesus put His blessing on Peter's notion. Peter knew Jesus intimately—he knew the mind of the Master. He knew that his desire wasn't an impertinent presumption, but just a longing to follow the Lord into the realm of the supernatural. Jesus said, "If anyone serves me, let him follow me; and where I am, there my servant will be also. If anyone serves me, him my Father will honor" (John 12:26).

This is why, when you and I do godly exploits, we can trust that we are in the will of God and that He in His goodness will honor them. This is the thought in the words of Jesus in Mark 11:24 when He said, "Whatever things you ask, when you pray, believe that you receive them, and you will have them." The same applies to John 15:7: "If you abide in Me, and My words abide in you, *you will ask what you desire, and it shall be done for you*" (italics added). Or the often misinterpreted Mark 11:23:

> For assuredly, I say to you, whoever says to this mountain, "Be removed and be cast into the sea," and does not doubt in his heart, but believes that those things he says will come to pass, he will have whatever he says. Therefore I say to you, whatever things you ask when you pray, believe that you receive them, and you will have them.

Does this mean that we need merely speak the words, "Mercedes Benz, diamond rings, fur coats," into the air through believing prayer, and God will give them to us? I don't think so. If our covetous heart has been crucified with Christ, our desire won't be for more, bigger, better, but that none perish. We seek first the Kingdom of God and His righteousness, and all these things will be added to us, if we need them. Scripture actually warns that a covetous prayer will not be answered: "You ask and do not receive, because you ask amiss, that you may spend it on your pleasures" (James 4:3).

Where No Oxen Are

A verse that ministered to my heart for years is a strange little Scripture in Proverbs 14:4. It is strange because on first seeing it, you wonder how it could inspire exploits for God. It merely says, "Where no oxen are, the trough is clean; but much increase comes by the strength of an ox."

Let me try to illustrate what this means to me: I proudly display a trough I have build out of high quality timber. When you ask when I will be putting oxen into it, I look disgusted and reply that I would never put dirty oxen into my clean trough, as they would only mess it up.

The trough may be clean with no oxen, but it is useless without them. In the same way, many won't do a thing for the Kingdom of God because they are afraid of making a mess. They want to keep things neat, tidy and uncomplicated. They don't want to take risks, so they don't do a thing for the Kingdom of God.

It goes without saying that we shouldn't move until we get a quickened word, or a *rhema*, from God in certain major decisions. For some years, I desired to set up what I called the Living Waters Free Christian Literature Distribution Ministries which, as the name suggests, is a ministry of providing free gospel literature for the body of Christ worldwide. To finance this I wanted to establish a Christian bookstore and use the profits for the ministry. I suggested the thought to a number of godly men who said the idea was good, but the timing was wrong.

One day, one of those men felt a strong impression that the time was right. That evening we prayed about it after family devotions, asking God to confirm it to us. The same evening, Sue and I began our own Bible reading from Proverbs 11:21. We had been reading through a portion each night, and the following verses so confirmed my desire failure to step out in faith would have been blatant mistrust in God. Within days we had our own Christian bookstore opposite the local bar. The bar had a glass frontage and if drinking patrons looked towards our window they could see the words, "He who believes on Me shall never thirst–Jesus."

For that decision, which meant a change of vocation, we waited for a rhema, but the Great Commission doesn't leave any option. It is a command and therefore doesn't need a special word of confirmation. I don't have to seek God to confirm His directive to "preach the Word, in season and out of season." With such a clear admonition, we should be able to say as David, "Once has God spoken, twice have I heard." We shouldn't neglect prayer and waiting on the Lord—we should pray as we go.

The Original Greek

For those of you who have trouble understanding the English translation, the original Greek meaning of "go into all the world and preach the gospel to every creature" (Mark

16:15) opens up some interesting thoughts. The word for "go" is very absorbing. It is *poreuomai*, meaning "go." The word "all" also carries with it gripping connotations. It is *hapas*, and actually means "all." And if that doesn't rivet you, look closely at the word "every." It is *pas*, and literally means "every." So when Jesus said, "Go into all the world and preach the gospel to every creature," to be true and faithful to the original text, what He was actually saying was "Go into all the world and preach the gospel to every creature." We are so fortunate to have access to knowledge like this.

Stunning Feet

Those who are obedient to the Great Commission will find that God will honor their desires:

> And whatever we ask we receive of Him, because we keep His commandments, and do those things that are pleasing in His sight. (1 John 3:22)

If anything is "pleasing in His sight," it is obedience to the Great Commission. God is so pleased with those who preach His Word and witness for the gospel, that He sees even the lowliest part of us as beautiful—"How beautiful are the feet of them that preach the gospel of peace." The Apostle Paul revealed the priority of his heart when he said, "To the weak, became I as weak, that I might gain the weak; I am made all things to all men, that I might by all means save some" (1 Cor. 9:22).

Our bus, the paper, the book and movie were just concepts to reach the lost, and God in His goodness and His condescension blessed them.

Those seeking a personal great commission need to go back to their relationship with Jesus and ask the question, "Do I know the heartbeat of my God?" If we don't know His will, the Bible says we are unwise—"Therefore do not be unwise, but understand what the will of the Lord is" (Eph. 5:17). Paul's prayer for the believer was that he would be "filled with the knowledge of His will" (Col. 1:9). The very reason God came to this earth in the person of Jesus Christ, and suffered on the cross, was for the salvation of the world. Has God lost His enthusiasm to see the lost saved? Has He changed His mind and is now willing that sinners perish? Is He now wanting worship without service? No, His will is that none perish, and that all come to repentance. To seek and save that which is lost is to flow in perfect harmony with the Father's will.

THREE

I Know a Diamond
When I See One!

In Dallas, Texas, W. A. Criswell, a Baptist legend who for more than fifty years preached a literal Bible and an uncompromising fundamentalism, said that the Southern Baptist Convention is declining and will be replaced as the major evangelical denomination in the United States. "I don't think we will ever split. I think we will erode . . . I think we will gradually acquiesce," Criswell said. "God will raise up somebody else to take our place." But he believes there are irreversible trends indicating that Southern Baptists as a whole are following the path of the United Methodist, Presbyterian and other mainline denominations that have emphasized soul-winning evangelism but have turned inward.

What he was saying in essence is, where has our get-up-and-go gone? Too many who profess to be Christians haven't got a get-up-and-go that has gone, because it was never there in the first place. The world can waste its time with its futility, but we have a mandate: "Let the dead bury their dead; but you go and preach the Kingdom of God" (Luke 9:60).

Watchman Nee, in his book, *The Spiritual Man* said:

> The passivity of the saint arises out of the non-use of his various talents. He has a mouth but refuses to talk because he hopes the Holy Spirit will talk through it. He has hands but will not engage them since he expects God to do it. He does not exercise any part of his person but waits for God to move him. He considers himself fully surrendered to God, so will no longer use any element of his being.

He continues by saying:

> They think their will must be canceled out and that they must become puppets. By falling into this state of inaction, the Christian now ceases from every activity. Indeed, he waits quietly all the time for some external force to activate him. And unless this force compels him to move he shall remain decidedly inert.

When Jesus ascended into heaven, it must have been a glorious sight. The angels said to the disciples that "this same Jesus will come in like manner." He ascended in the same manner in which He will come, so there must have been "clouds, power and great glory." When the disciples were caught up in the glory of the Ascension, the two angels appeared and brought them back to this world with the words, "Men of Galilee, why do you stand gazing up into Heaven?"

We haven't been saved to stand and "gaze up to heaven," but to take the light to those who sit in the dark shadow of death. How can any person, who professes to have the love of God in them, sit in passivity while sinners die daily and go to hell? Paul said, "Woe to me if I preach not the gospel!" We cannot but speak that which we have seen and heard.

A friend of mine couldn't get a clear word from God as to whether or not to go to New Guinea with a team to both construct a church building and to evangelize. Then he heard about a man who was waiting on God for a long time. He waited and waited . . . then he died. So, my friend decided to go before he died and had an incredible time.

Honors and Big Prizes

Elbert Hubbard once said:

> The world bestows its big prizes, both in honors and money, for but one thing, and that is initiative. And what is initiative? I'll tell you: it is doing the right thing without being told!

If you want people to appreciate you, and heap praise upon you, then do the right thing without being told. If a friend drops into a seat, exhausted after a day's work, and you know he loves a hot beverage when he is tired, then make

him one without being told. You will be praised.
David did the "right thing" when he heard
Goliath blaspheming. Peter did the right thing
when he wanted to be with Jesus, and you and
I do the right thing when we seek and save that
which is lost.

With that thought in mind, look at the new
covenant (conversion) in Hebrews 8:10: "I will
put my laws within their mind and write them
on their hearts."

The word "hearts" is *kardia*, and means "the
thoughts or feelings." Look at how the Living
Bible paraphrases the verse: "I will write My
laws within their minds *so that they will know
what I want them to do without My even telling
them*" (italics added).

Have you ever noticed how Luke begins his
gospel? Does he say that God told him to write
it? No, he merely says, "It seemed good to me"
to write it. Luke had a perfect understanding of
the life and ministry of Jesus, so he put pen to
paper, and God blessed his labor.

We need to "go to the ant, consider her
ways, and be wise, which having no guide, over-
seer or ruler, provides her meat in the summer,
and gathers her food in the harvest." In California, you don't need to go to the ant, the ant
comes to you. Ants don't need to be continually
motivated to work. They are full of initiative, in
fact, in my conclusive studies of ants, I have
never seen one taking a rest. The only still ant
you will see is a dead ant. They are maniacs for
work, and God points to them as our example.

Look at what Ernest Newman said:

> The great composer does not set to work
> because he is inspired, but becomes inspired
> because he is working. Beethoven, Wagner,
> Bach and Mozart settled down day after
> day to the job in hand with as much regu-
> larity as an accountant settles down each
> day with his figures. They didn't waste time
> waiting for inspiration.

The revealed will of God in Scripture should
be our inspiration. If God has purchased the
car, filled it with gas, paid the insurance, given
us the license, sat us in the driver's seat, shown
us our destination, started the engine and told
us to go, should He now have to push the car?

Peter used initiative in Acts chapter 3 when
he prayed for the lame man. He did the right
thing without being told. He didn't have to pray
and seek God's will, because he knew it already.
He knew that Jesus "went about doing good,
and healing those who were vexed by the devil."
In verse 12 of the same chapter, we see that
when the miracle of healing took place, "all the
people ran together to them . . . and when Peter saw it, he answered the people." A modern
version says, "And when Peter *saw his opportunity*" (italics added). Peter didn't pray and see
if it was God's will to preach the gospel to every
creature, he saw an opportunity, and used his
initiative and preached to them.

Do you remember the incident in Acts 16:6
where the disciples were heading for Asia, and
God told them not to go there? What does that

show us? It shows that the disciples didn't have a "word from the Lord" to evangelize in Asia. If they had prayed, "Lord, do you want us to preach the gospel in Asia?" and God had directed them to go there, it means that He then changed His mind. Rather, the disciples merely obeyed the command to "Go into all the world, and preach the gospel to every creature," and God, in His faithfulness had directed their steps by saying, "Not Asia at this time."

If there is one thing Satan seeks to kill, steal and destroy, it is man's initiative and creativity, especially in the area of evangelism. When people say to me, "You are very creative," I agree and say, "My Father is very creative. Look at Genesis chapter 1." God is Creativity itself, and, I say it reverently, He is full of initiative. God took the initiative in the beginning when He spoke creation into being. When Adam fell, so did his direct contact with the Father, but now you and I have the mind of Christ. We have access to the incredibly infinite intellect of Almighty God, and we can let His creativity flow through us.

Left Foot of Fellowship

You may be asking the question as to what you can do in a practical way to reach people for the Kingdom of God. There are a number of evangelical organizations you may like to join. I was in Gideons International for seven years, until I became a pastor, as they don't allow pastors to be involved, only lay people. It is such a blessing to be involved in an organization that gives away copies of God's Word. Then there is Youth With A Mission, Youth For Christ, Full Gospel Businessmen's Association, Campus Crusade For Christ, Women's Aglow and many others you could become involved in. Perhaps you could invest in a small advertisement in the personal column of your local paper saying something like "Find reality, read John 8:31-32." Get a cost quote before you commit yourself. I wanted to buy a full page in the *Los Angeles Times* during the Persian Gulf War in 1991. I thought it would be around six thousand dollars and figured I could probably raise that sort of money.

I called the *Times* and the gentleman gave me the cost: "A full page is $61,023." I thought he had slipped an extra number in by mistake. Wrong. I dropped that idea quickly.

Perhaps you could visit a hospital once a week, with the purpose of finding and befriending someone who doesn't normally have visitors. If you have a flare for drama, start a drama group. How about writing a tract? Don't say, "But I can't write," say, "I can do all things through Christ who strengthens me." Write out your testimony, and have a friend or two read it and give their opinion. Then print out the edited copy and have it typeset at your local printers. Remember to get quotes before you do anything, so that you won't get burned. When it is printed, keep copies in your wallet or purse to give to old friends or people you meet, with the words, "You may like to read this when you have a moment. I wrote it myself." Put copies into the envelope when paying bills.

Back in the late seventies, I had forty to fifty children in our garage every Friday for a twenty-minute Good-time Club. I remember praying that God would send me someone who could play a guitar to give the music a bit of a lift. One Friday evening, my brother-in-law walked into our living room knowing nothing of my prayer, and said, "For some reason I feel the Lord wants me to give you my guitar." I hadn't thought of me. I was never able to play a guitar, but now I can do all things through Christ who strengthens me (I just have trouble convincing those in ear shot).

You could easily start a club through your local church. When I decided to start mine, I just took a marker pen and wrote, "KIDS CLUB, FRIDAY 4 P.M., (ADDRESS), CANDY, PRIZES, STORIES AND SONGS," gave out photocopies at a school gate, and had a crowd of children eager to learn about the things of God. Nowadays, with all the allegations and accusations of child molestation, and so forth, it would be wise to have both male and female leaders. Start with a firm hand, sing some lively songs, tell a Bible story, teach a memory verse, give out some candy, then tell the kids, "It's all over, see you next week." If the children don't say "Ohhhhhh!" you've probably gone on too long and they may not be back the following week. I found twenty minutes was adequate for most.

Sometimes talented Christians don't feel right about using their gift of music or writing, or the like, to reach the unsaved. It is often because of their own pride, that their conscience is condemning them, and not God. This happens regularly with counterculture people who become Christians. Their conscience will not allow them to eat meat. After some time they come across a Scripture such as 1 Timothy 4:3-4, which says that God has created all foods "to be received with thanksgiving by them who believe and know the truth. For every creature of God is good, and nothing is to be refused, if it is received with thanksgiving." Immediately their conscience is released by understanding the Word of God.

When we understand the emphasis which the Word of God places upon evangelism, we should humble ourselves, thank God for the gift He has given us, then use it for His glory. If you have no apparent talents, visit an old people's home, or ask your pastor if you can help in any way within the local church. Do something for God. Desire to do nothing, and God will give you the desires of your heart.

Dig in Your Own Soil

An old Arab once told a poor man of the beauty of diamonds. He told him that if he possessed just a handful of sparklers, he would never want for anything ever again. He could have whatever he desired in life. From that time on, the poor man began to dream about diamonds. He spent every moment thinking about those glittering gems. Finally, he was so consumed by that dream, he left his home and began a search for his dream. Wherever he went he would dig for diamonds.

Years passed, until that disappointed poor man flung himself into the sea and committed suicide.

The old Arab visited the poor man's home not knowing of his death. As he walked into the living room he noticed a rock on the mantelpiece and said, "Where did you get that diamond . . . is the poor man back?" Those in the house said that it was just a rock they had found out in the back yard. The Arab picked it up in his trembling hand and said, "I know a diamond when I see one—where did you get it?" They rushed out to the back yard and began digging in its white sands, and found diamond, after diamond, after diamond. Thus began the Golconda Diamond Mines, which exceeded the Kimberley Mines in value!

You don't need to chase around the world searching for the illusive and sparkling diamonds of the will of God; just begin to cultivate your own back yard. The Bible says, "a good man shall be satisfied from himself." Start digging for those gems of creativity, and then do something for the Kingdom of God.

When John Wesley was asked what he would do with his life if he knew that he would die at midnight the next day, his answer was something like this:

I would just carry on with what I am doing.
I will arise at 5:00 A.M. for prayer, then take
a house meeting at 6.00 A.M. At 12 noon, I
will be preaching at an open-air. At 3:00
P.M. I have another meeting in another town.
At 6:00 P.M. I have a house meeting, at
10:00 P.M. I have a prayer meeting and at
12:00 midnight, I would go to be with my
Lord.

If we knew we were to die at twelve o'clock
tomorrow night, would we have to step up our
evangelistic program, or could we in all good
conscience carry on just as we are?

It would seem that there are only three types
of people in this world—the jawbone, the wishbone and the backbone. The jawbone says he
will do something, one day. He never puts his
muscle where his mouth is. He prays about
things, but never does them. His conscience
stirs him to prayer, but the warmth of his comfort zone stifles his good intentions, because his
own well-being is more important to him.

The wishbone gazes with starry eyes at his
godly heroes and wishes he could be like them.
His is a world of dreams. Like the jawbone, he
is easily divided from his goals. He wishes he
could preach, write, pray, sing and dance. Yet,
no one ever did anything without doing something. An aspiration will only become a realization with perspiration. If he wants to see revival, he should stop wishing and start fishing,
but his dreams are not fuel enough to motivate
him.

In contrast, the backbone sees Goliath and runs towards him. He breaks out of the comfort zone of apathy, warmth and security. He leaves the fat cat of indifference sleeping by the fire. He walks on water while others sit in the safety of the boat. He uses what he has to do the will of His Heavenly Father. He knows his God and does exploits.

FOUR

The Doctor with No B.A.

There were once three doctors in the city of Adam. One day a deathly disease broke out in the metropolis, and authorities traced the cause to water from nearby Lake Iniquitous. Everyone was affected because the lake was the only source of the city's water supply.

The name of one of the physicians was Dr. Ian Dulgence. Unfortunately, Dr. Dulgence was a man whose sole motive for entering the medical profession was questionable. He saw his vocation purely as a lucrative means of income. As far as he was concerned, his patients' diseases were nothing more than the means to a wage, so he was never genuinely interested in their welfare, only his own.

The second doctor was Dr. I.G. Norance (B.A.). Dr. Norance had a good and honest heart. The reason he entered the profession was for the relief of suffering humanity. However, this doctor found to his dismay, that even though his patients listened intently to his advice, they would never finish the prescribed medicine he gave them. In fact, he became very discouraged because many of his patients went back to drinking from the polluted lake. This mystified the good doctor, as he earnestly wanted to see his patients cured.

The third doctor was Dr. "Bib" Lical (B.A.). Bib (an affectionate nickname given to him when he was a child) also had a good and honest heart, and if there was any difference between him and Dr. Norance, it was the fact that he would always do things according to the medical instruction book. Never would he deviate from the directions given in the manual, even down to his bedside manner.

This difference between the two could be seen in the way they dealt with their patients. Dr. Norance lacked knowledge as to how to effectively deal with the disease which resulted from drinking from the lake. He didn't appreciate the importance of the fact that each patient needed a shot to kill the infection before giving him medicine which was to be taken orally. His lack of knowledge as to why the patient should have the shot caused him to merely give the medicine alone. Besides, he disliked seeing anyone in pain, and the needle did cause pain. Rather than labor on the consequences of drinking from Lake Iniquitous, he would speak of more pleasant things. He didn't want to alarm the patient, as he considered fear to be detrimental to the patient's welfare.

Bib however, saw fear as something that

could work for the long-term good of the suf-
ferer. While talking with his patient, he would
take the time to educate him by making sure he
understood why he was ill, that it was solely
because he had been drinking the water from
Lake Iniquitous. He would show him highly magnified pictures of the virus, and watch his
patient's eyes widen as he saw the death-causing
bacteria that were invisible to the naked eye.
He carefully explained that the disease produced
tiny worms that would eat their way through
the stomach linings, then through the bowels,
eventually spreading poison throughout the
whole body, bringing about an excruciating
death. In fact, Dr. Lical didn't even hint that
there was a cure to the affliction until he felt
the patient understood the seriousness of his
plight. Did the doctor do this because he wanted
the patient to squirm in fear at the thought of
what would happen to him? No. He knew that
if he didn't see the seriousness of his dilemma,
he would not continue with the prescribed
medicine and would eventually die. Not one of
Dr. Lical's patients went back to drinking from
Lake Iniquitous.

Within the church, we have three different
types of professing Christians. First, we have
the self-indulgent "believer." He made a commitment to the Savior under the sound of the
modern gospel. He was told that Jesus was a
means of self-improvement, that He would give
him an abundant life of peace, joy, happiness,
and all other good things. Despite his practice

of the Christian life through fellowship, worship and prayer, he is still in his sins, because he has never been awakened by the Law of God in the hand of the Spirit. He cares only for himself and has no zeal at all for the lost. He looks at God as a means to his own ends, rather than Lord of his life. He calls Jesus Lord, but doesn't do the things He tells him. He is the "backslider in heart," filled with his own ways rather than the ways of God. He doesn't have his B.A.—he's not born again.

The second doctor is typical of the believer who is truly born again. He is a genuine convert, but he is in ignorance as to how to effectively reach the lost. He has been unwittingly shaped by twentieth century evangelical tradition. He preaches Christ crucified, repentance and faith, thinking that is complete biblical evangelism. However, his message lacks the Law to bring the "knowledge of sin." He also neglects to mention future punishment, so his converts don't stick, mainly because they are "his" converts, rather than God's. He doesn't see the need to follow the example of Jesus, and use the needle of the Law to penetrate the flesh for the saving medicine of the gospel. He thinks that it is biblical to draw people to Christ through the promise of a rich, full, abundant and wonderful life, rather than driving them to the Savior with the Law of God, as did Spurgeon, Wesley, Whitefield, Moody, Finney, Luther and others God so greatly used to reach the lost. He gives the patient the cure before convincing him that he has the disease, and so the medicine of the gospel runs off his flesh and is unable to do its saving work. In his zeal without knowledge, he circumnavigates the divine means of producing contrition. He doesn't use the Law to convince the sinner that he has sinned against God, so there is therefore no "godly sorrow" that "works repentance."

Dr. Bib Lical however, is the Christian who has gained light on biblical rather than traditional evangelism. He knows that those who drink in iniquity like water have a disease which has ten clear symptoms. Sin is transgression of the Law (1 John 3:4), and the Ten Commandments tell the sinner what sin is (Rom. 7:13). He realizes that he must convince the sinner that he has the disease of sin, and he cannot do this without the Law (Rom. 7:7). If he isn't first "convinced of the Law as a transgressor" (James 2:9), he will eventually use the grace of God as an occasion of the flesh; he won't continue taking the cure. The Law must penetrate the flesh and make a way for the gospel that is able to save his soul.

The Christian who knows that biblical evangelism is Law to the proud and grace to the humble, will take the time to open up the commandments as Jesus did, so that the sinner will see the seriousness of his plight. He will not be afraid to use Scriptures that take away his sense of well-being such as, "fear Him who has power to cast both your body and soul into Hell" (Matt. 10:28), or "It is a fearful thing to fall into the

hands of the Living God" (Heb. 10:31). He knows
that the effect, if used in conjunction with the
Law and the conviction of the Holy Spirit, will
result in the sinner seeing the seriousness of the
disease of sin, and he will then take the cure of
the gospel with deep appreciation and gratitude. The Christian who has evangelical zeal
with knowledge lets the arrows of God's Law
pierce the sinner deeply and waits for the hand
of God's conviction to press him down (Ps. 38:2)
until he says with the psalmist, "There is no
soundness in my flesh because of Your anger,
nor any health in my bones because of my sin.
For my iniquities have gone over my head; like
a heavy burden they are too heavy for me." It is
only then that the sinner will "labor" and become "heavy laden" and seek the Savior to find
rest to his soul.

The Abundant Life

Still, the question may arise, Why not use
the fact that Christians have a full and happy
life, to draw people to the Savior? The answer
is clear. It is not biblical. Nowhere in Scripture
do you find Jesus, Paul or any of the disciples
telling people that Jesus will make them happy.
But what about the "abundant life" Jesus said
He had come to bring? True, the Christian life
is full. Study the life of Paul and see if you think
he was bored while being stoned, shipwrecked,
beaten and whipped. Check out what happened
to the disciples when persecution hit. Read *Foxes
Book of Martyrs*, or study the life of John Wesley

and see a man with a mission. He took the Great Commission seriously, and was always abounding in the work of the Lord, knowing that his labor was not in vain.

But, doesn't the Bible say, "Happy are the people whose God is the Lord"? (Ps. 144:15). Yes, and of course it is true. When a nation has God as their Lord, and obeys the Ten Commandments, then there is no theft, lying, murder, greed, lust, and other sin. In fact, the first of the Ten Commandments sets the stage for the rest. It begins with the words, "I am the Lord your God," and when a people have God as their sovereign, they are happy—as happened with Israel under Solomon. But when there are Christians in a nation whose God is not their Lord, there will be persecution, if they are living "godly in Christ Jesus."

Christians who are in ignorance as to biblical evangelism will be drawn into the unscriptural methods of modern evangelism, as I was for many years.

Tombstone Evangelism

I spoke to a lady once who had lived in both Texas and California, and she said she preferred tornadoes to earthquakes. The reason she gave was that you had no choice when in an earthquake, but if you could see a tornado moving across the horizon, you knew you were safe. There was, however, one drawback. "But," she said, "if it remains still, you are in big trouble!" If the twister didn't seem to be moving, it was actually heading for you.

Christians are aware of the tornado of Judgment Day. We can see that great and terrible day moving across the horizon toward unregenerate humanity. We know that we are safe in Christ, but the ungodly are totally unaware that it is heading towards them. They are not alarmed because the tornado doesn't seem to be heading in their direction. They say in their hearts, "The Lord does not see, nor does the God of Jacob understand." But we know that the justice of Almighty God is gathering wrath, like a massive tornado, storing up fury that will be revealed on the day of wrath, and God has given us the sobering job of warning them.

I was encouraged to hear that Paris Reidhead, a well-known and respected Bible teacher who went to be with the Lord in 1992, had written across his tombstone the words, "How shall we escape if we neglect so great salvation!" He knew his Bible enough to see its message to this sinful world.

Those sincere Christians who are concerned about alarming the sinner, are like Dr. Ignorance. They need to see that fear works for the welfare of the sinner, not to his detriment. If he doesn't understand the full and dreadful consequences of sin, he will continue to go back to the waters of iniquity. We don't revel in the trepidation of our hearers, but we see that it is the way of the Spirit of God, that there may be a fleeing from the wrath to come.

Garry Ansdell, the senior pastor at my home church, told me of a distressed mother who brought her seven-year-old child to him for counsel. The boy had been stealing substantial amounts of cash from his mother's purse and seemed to show no remorse when confronted by her. In her frustration, she took the child to the pastor, and when he confronted the boy, there was only silence on the child's part.

Some sleight of hand tricks seemed to brighten the sullen face of the boy, but when he was told that he needed to repent and ask both the Lord and his mother to forgive him, the lad remained decidedly mute. So, the pastor picked up the phone and said he was calling the police to have them come and pick him up. The boy's eyes widened, but there was still no sign of sorrow. As the pastor slowly dialed the number, he looked at the boy and asked if he knew how to pray. He shook his head, so the pastor led him in a prayer, thinking within his own mind that the boy still wasn't truly sorry. However, when the child opened his eyes there were tears of contrition, and he then turned to his mother and said, "I'm sorry." It was fear of the consequences, coupled with the conviction of his conscience, that produced sorrow. He was a thief and his conscience smote him.

As impenitent sinners sit before us, we need not hesitate to summon the Law. Sometimes, we may have to dial through all the Ten Commandments before there is any reaction. Jesus called the Law into action to awaken a "certain lawyer" in Luke 10:25. He actually dialed six of the Ten Commandments for the rich young ruler in Luke 18:18.

I have heard it said that the Ten Commandments are like a balloon—"one hole destroys all of them." If we offend in one point, we are guilty of all. However, the analogy would be better fitting if it was said that man is like a balloon, and the Ten Commandments are like ten sharp needles. Infringe one, and you are the one who perishes. If we didn't transgress the Law through sin, our lives wouldn't be a transient "vapor, that appears for a moment, then vanishes away."

Yawnese, the International Language

In the early nineties in Palm Bay, Florida, three youths picked up a video camera, and in a sense of bravado, filmed each other and boasted that they had committed a number of burglaries in the area. They then laughed, broke the video cassette and threw it into a river.

Some time later, two men found the cassette and were stirred by curiosity. They repaired it, and after screening it and seeing its contents, gave the cassette to the police. The guilt of the youths was so evident, they didn't even go to trial to defend themselves and were jailed for many years.

When graphic evidence is produced in court which shows absolute guilt, there is an appropriate legal expression. The literal interpretation for the Latin phrase used to describe such an incident is "the thing speaks for itself." That will be the case on Judgment Day for sinful humanity. Every transgression has been recorded by the omniscient eye of a holy Creator "who will bring to judgment every secret thing, whether it is good or evil" (Eccles. 12:14). When Christians forget that fact, they lose sight of their priorities.

Early in 1993, I had the privilege of spending some time with Leonard Ravenhill. The well-respected preacher was eighty-five years old and took the time to share with me some of the wisdom God has given him over the years. He said that there are only two sorts of people on this earth—"those who are dead to sin, and those who are dead in sin." Then the aged man of God said, "If God would give me one more chance to preach on a world tour, I would speak of the judgment of believers, the judgment of sinners, and the judgment of preachers." I trust that you have similar urgent priorities and still have opportunity, energy and motivation to warn sinners to flee from the wrath to come. May God give it to each of us if we are lacking.

The result of ignoring the fact of Judgment Day, is that there are many pastors who haven't motivation enough to motivate. There is no alarm in the pulpit, and therefore no alarm in the pew. If God is the pastor's ultimate employer, it's my prayer that He will fire them—not *from* their pulpits, but fire them *in* their pulpits. Enthusiasm for the lost is contagious, and it can spread like wildfire in moments from the pulpit to the pew, if the wind of the Spirit blows that way.

I spent some time in Minneapolis, where the lifestyle is radically different from southern California. In winter, the sidewalks have snow piled up along the edges of them because it is the legal responsibility of the business owners to keep them clear.

After having a meal at a restaurant, I walked up to the counter and heard the man I was with say, "There is ice on your sidewalk. I fell over while carrying my child and he hit his head on the ground!" The lady behind the counter was extremely apologetic, because it was the restaurant's responsibility not only to clear the sidewalk of snow, but if conditions produced an invisible sheet of ice on the sidewalk, they were to scatter salt on it. It was then I discovered an interesting property of salt. The scattered salt generates heat and actually melts the ice. That's how Christians can have a salty influence among those brethren who have grown cold towards the lost. Our enthusiasm for evangelism can melt their icy hearts.

Some time ago, I contacted a radio station and asked if they had recordings of noises such as horns honking, doors slamming, and the like. When I found that they had such a recording, I located yawns on it, and had them duplicate ten minutes worth. I duplicated those ten minutes several times to make a one hour cassette tape. Just for fun, I had a tape jacket printed and called the tape "Yawnees . . . the international language—60 minutes of pure, genuine, non-stop yawns." It had a variety of uses. It was the insomniac's dream. It was also invaluable for those late night visitors that won't leave. One could quietly put the tape on and watch as the guests began to yawn and look at their watches.

I noticed that seeing a yawn can start a yawn, and hearing one has the same effect. In fact, just reading about yawning can trigger the desire. A congregation can detect a yawn in the pulpit. If the pastor is lacking in zeal for the unsaved, invariably, so will they. Evangelism to them will be one big yawn. The preference in the pulpit will determine the priority of the pew. If you don't believe it, listen to how many congregations pray, and you will often hear the same phrases, expressions and even personal characteristics of the pastor. If he focuses merely on doctrines of self-improvement, so will the flock.

There are however, numbers of pastors who have not lost sight of the Great Commission. In January of 1993, I was invited to the Dallas area by a pastor who asked me to speak at his Sunday church services. He was a little disappointed because he had invited me to go out witnessing on the Saturday night, and a thunderstorm arrived about an hour after my plane landed. I had never seen anything like it. There was such intensity of lightning, that every few seconds, the sky would light up like noonday. Then it rained cats and dogs (they were everywhere). It looked like we wouldn't have the opportunity to go outdoors, so we decided that we would go to witness at a mall.

The pastor was very gracious and gave me the choice as to whether or not I wanted to go witnessing, saying he would understand if I wanted to rest after the flight. I could either rest up in my hotel, or with the help of God, seek and save the lost. The temptation was there to rest, but I of course chose the latter.

The words "lifestyle evangelism" have come to mean to many that we merely live a Christian life in contrast to that of the ungodly, in the hope that some day they will be drawn to our light. But, if we want to see people saved, we must try and save them. Who could ever stand passively on a river bank hoping a drowning person will somehow be drawn to us so that we could then rescue them? The Scriptures use a more fearful analogy—fire rather than water: "Others save with fear, pulling them from the fire" (Jude 1:23). This pastor was putting legs to his prayers and was going to the sinner.

It was dinner time, and he dropped me off at the entrance of a restaurant while he parked the car. Then, a few minutes later, we were seated in a warm and dry atmosphere as a waitress made us feel at home. As she began to walk away, I said, "Here's a little gift for you," and handed her a glistening penny with the Ten Commandments pressed into it. She took the penny and, predictably, asked what it was. When I told her, she said sincerely, "Thank you very much."

When another waitress brought the menus to us, I gave her an I.Q. tract, and said that she might like to try it when she had a moment to spare. A few minutes later, another waitress came and asked if she could buy a penny. I gave her one, then the first waitress returned and said she had failed the I.Q. test. It was then that I saw another waitress standing behind the pastor. She smiled, so I gave her a penny. When she was very open to Christian things, I gave her a signed copy of one of my books, for which she seemed very grateful.

Notice that we didn't just sit there hoping that our light would draw sinners to us, but we made an effort to reach out. This is "lifestyle evangelism" as it should be. If people are drowning in their sins everywhere we go, then we should make an effort to save them everywhere we go.

As we paid our bill in the lobby, four or five members of the staff stood around us and asked us questions such as who we were. To let our light shine is merely a matter of letting the love of God flow through us, rather than stop in us.

When we came out of the restaurant, the storm had passed. So the pastor gave me a choice as to where we could now go—either to the "cowboy" part of town, the "prostitute" place or the "punk" area. Somehow I didn't feel like trying to witness to guys twice my size in high-heel boots and ten-gallon hats. The last place I want to visit when I am away from Sue would be a prostitute area, especially in the light of so many preachers falling, or diving, into sexual sin. I remember feeling unspiritual years ago, when I heard of a well-known preacher who would boldly go into brothels and witness to prostitutes. Here was one man who seemed to be able to keep the red blood in his veins cool. It turned out that he eventually fell sexually and left his wife for another woman.

Moths should stay away from flames, so, without any hesitation, I chose Punksville. Punks are always a challenge. For some reason I feel safe with a woman who has "hate" written on her cheeks, black lipstick, weird clothes, filthy language, semishaven scalp, a rooster hairstyle, orange hair and pins through her nose.

Unfortunately, we got lost and ended up in the Dallas "cowboy" area. As we made our way toward some very loud music, the wind blew something into the pastor's eye, and it lodged under his contact lens. It was so painful, we decided to go back to his car so that he could take the contacts out.

As we turned around, another gust of wind blew the hat off a man who was walking towards us. He was accompanied by a very pretty woman in her midtwenties. As Mike and the man ran after the hat, the woman lunged at me and, to my unbelief, threw her arms around my neck and tried to force her lips onto mine. I screamed and prized the woman's arms from around my neck. Then I handed her a penny with the Ten Commandments pressed into it and told her what it was. Mike and I witnessed briefly to both the man and Potifer's wife, then we went back to the car and prayed for them both. As we sat there, I felt I should somehow try to reassure the pastor, so I said, "That's the first time anything like that has ever happened to me." He looked back at me mournfully and said, with tongue in cheek, "It's never happened to me!"

We didn't find any punks that night, but we had a good time witnessing to a group of about a dozen youths. We entered a mall and gave I.Q. tracts to two teen-age boys. They did the tests and couldn't believe they failed them. One ran off and returned with two friends so that they too could feel the humiliation of failure. When they blew it, I said, "You can't trust your eyes . . . watch this," and did some sleight of hand, which sent the same youth off with eyes like saucers to get some more of his friends.

Suddenly, we had about a dozen young men watching my every move and listening to my every word. Even the security guard watched intently. When I told the young men I was a Christian and warned them that they had to face God on Judgment Day, they stayed and listened. We witnessed to them for a few minutes, shook their hands and moved to another part of the mall.

Perhaps you are thinking that you could never do such a thing, yet all you need is a little love to motivate you and a little knowledge to equip you. We have a package which has two of the most incredible sleight of hand tricks, that will astound the person you are witnessing to. It is called "Getting the Earlobe Using Sleight of

Hand." Write to us for details. Anyone with half a brain and two hands can do these tricks, and it has so much potential evangelically, because it will make your listeners respect you, and therefore listen to what you have to say.

Despite the loose woman, the lack of punks and the security guards who told me I needed a permit to do any more tricks, or to even hand out tracts, we had a good time. That night as I lay my head on my pillow, I smiled a lot, thanked God that I broke out of my comfort zone and prayed for those who we had been privileged to witness to.

The Good Wine

One of the most fearful instances of someone breaking out of his comfort zone is Stephen. The Bible tells us that he was a man full of the Holy Spirit and faith. He was respected in his office as a minister of the gospel of salvation, was wise, had a good reputation and could have therefore lived a comfortable and abundant life as a Christian, enjoying the comforts of a happy family life. But he didn't. Stephen loved God, he loved truth and he loved sinners enough to preach the truth to them.

We pick up the story in Acts chapter 6 when the twelve disciples decided that they didn't want to neglect prayer and the Word of God to serve tables, so they found seven men to do the job, one of whom was Stephen. The Scriptures tell us the "the number of the disciples multiplied greatly," because men like Stephen didn't confine their ministry to serving tables. They had their priorities sorted out, preached the gospel and God confirmed His Word with signs following (verse 8).

However, this didn't please Satan. Whenever a servant of God serves the truth in the court of the world, the devil is going to return the serve with vengeance. When professing godly Jews couldn't resist the wisdom by which Stephen spoke, the father of lies provided some more of his children to distort his words, and say that he was speaking blasphemy. Suddenly, Stephen found himself standing before the council and his slanderous accusers. All it took was, "Are these things so?" to push Stephen's evangelical button. Beginning at Abraham, he recounted the history of Israel, saying nothing offensive to them until verse 51. He saved the good wine until last. His sermon ended with a number of relevant points for his congregation to consider:

1. His hearers were stubborn.
2. They were unholy.
3. They were spiritually deaf.
4. They and their fathers resisted the Holy Spirit.
5. They were the sons of murderers.
6. They were betrayers and murderers of "the Just One."

Stephen disqualified himself from the Popular Preacher of the Year award. Then from his breast, he produced what Charles Spurgeon called his "ablest auxiliary." This was his greatest weapon—the Law of God. The Jews were proud of the thought that they had kept the Law, and by saying they had broken it, Stephen touched the apple of their evil eye. He climaxed his sermon by saying that they "have received the Law by the direction of angels and have not kept it" (verse 53). He pointed to the divine plumline to show his hearers how crooked they were. This made them foam at the mouth like mad dogs. They were cut to the heart, then "gnashed at him with their teeth."

Their reaction didn't seem to worry Stephen too much. He was so full of the Holy Spirit, he was gazing at a vision of Jesus standing at the right hand of God, and said, "Look, I see the heavens opened and the Son of Man standing at the right hand of God" (Acts 7:56).

Another puissant poke in the apple of their widened eyes. They cried out with a loud voice, stopped their ears, ran at him with one accord and dashed his body with great stones until he breathed his last breath of this contemptible world's air.

Stephen's sermon was a little different from that of the modern preacher. He failed to mention "Christ crucified" or the fact that God loved them. He didn't even mention grace. He didn't give that which is holy to the dogs. Neither did he woo his hearers with soft words, low lights and soul-stirring music. If he had, he wouldn't have offended a soul, and could have remained in his comfort zone. Devil, demon, Jew and Gentile would have smiled. Stephen's "decisions" were nonexistent. By modern standards, he had failed to reap any souls. The only decision made by his listeners was a unified decision to spill the preacher's blood.

Stephen's boldness so stirred one hearer that he reinforced a resolve that would change the course of the Christian history. Saul of Tarsus was so disgusted by what he saw and heard, he decided he would wipe the Church off the face of the earth.

Stephen's precious blood was the first to be shed as ground work for the Church that would follow. He knew from experience the truth of the hymn writer that would be penned many centuries later, "Love so amazing, so divine, demands my life, my all."

Evangelical Utopia

Every time you open your mouth for God, you are breaking out of your comfort zone, you are taking a risk for the sake of the Kingdom. I was once sitting on a plane, relaxing and enjoying the flight. There were only a few people on board, so I had plenty of room to spread out and do some writing. I had good food, cool water, a pillow and a tray for my computer. Happiness. It was a relief when no one sat next to me, so instead of getting into the "battle of the fear of man," I could relax in comfort.

After about three hours, I went for a walk to the restroom, and on the way back to my seat, I passed a man in his late twenties who looked a little bored, so I gave him an I.Q. tract. When he failed two different tracts, I sat down next to him and told him that we fail because our eyes are easily fooled. Then I did a sleight of hand trick that widened his eyes. He did the spiritual I.Q. test on side two of the tract and proved to be very open to the things of God, so I spent about twenty minutes witnessing to him. Then I prayed with him, that his conscience would remind him of his past sins, that he would see the seriousness of his transgression, that the Lord would grant him light until he came to a point of peace with God. I also prayed that God would bless him and his family and keep them in health. We parted with a handshake and his other hand filled with literature.

To break out of the warmth of your comfort zone means to risk the ice-cold air of rejection, resentment and even hatred. But when you leave a warm room to venture into the cold, how nice and cozy the room seems when you get back. When I sat back down in my seat, I had the heartwarming knowledge that I had pleased God and done what I should as a Christian. If you have a good day for the Lord by being a true and faithful witness, when you go to bed at night, you will glow, knowing that this was a day of victory for you and defeat for the devil, because you broke free from the shackles of the fear of man.

The Stubborn King

Think of how many times Jeremiah warned King Zedekiah about the coming judgment of

God upon Israel. The king was party to personal warnings as well as public. I have never taken the time to count, but I wouldn't be surprised if he was warned over a dozen times. The batteries were removed from the smoke detector of the king's conscience, and one day, he was trapped by the fire.

Look at what happened when judgment came:

> Then the king of Babylon killed the sons of Zedekiah before his eyes in Riblah . . . moreover he put out Zedekiah's eyes, and bound him with bronze fetters to carry him off to Babylon. And the Chaldeans burned the king's house with fire and the houses of the people with fire, and broke down the walls of Jerusalem. (Jer. 39:6–8)

I wonder what the king thought about as he stumbled in the blackness, bound with chains. Perhaps his thoughts were of the last thing he saw—the unspeakable agony of seeing his own beloved sons butchered before his eyes. Perhaps the words of Jeremiah flashed before his tormented mind, warning him that all Israel (including his sons) could have been saved if he had obeyed the voice of the Lord. We can't begin to imagine the remorse.

How this typifies the ungodly who have been bound by the bronze fetters of sin, "taken captive by the devil to do his will." We warn them that there is judgment coming (both temporal and eternal) to those who live for the devil, but most remain in unbelief. Their master is he who came to "kill, steal and destroy." He blinds the "minds of them who believe not, lest the light of the glorious gospel of Christ should shine unto them." Like Zedekiah's sons, so many see their own sons and daughters die before their very eyes. AIDS, and other sin-related diseases, as well as alcohol, drugs and suicide, kill many before their time. Multitudes give themselves to the burning fires of sexual lust, and so the devil breaks down the walls of a whole nation.

Yet, there is still time to warn many, praying that God will open their understanding. God told Jeremiah to tell an Ethiopian called Ebed-Melech that God would deliver him from judgment. He said,

> "For I will surely deliver you, and you shall not fall by the sword; but your life shall be as a prize to you, because you have put your trust in Me," says the Lord. (Jer. 39:18)

This is the message we are to deliver. He who keeps his life will lose it, but those that trust in the Lord will be safe on that day. On the Day of Judgment, the sword of the Word of God will not fall upon him, because it fell on the Savior two thousand years ago. The name Ebed-Melech means "servant of a king." Those who are servants of the King will be true to the commission given them and carry out His every command.

FIVE

Running on Water

I had to drive about six miles each day to the heart of the city to preach the gospel. My old car's mileage had been "around the clock," and it had a habit of boiling over regularly. We made enquiries about a better vehicle, but after hearing of the finance needed, we decided to resort to prayer. The only way we would get one was if God provided it miraculously.

A few months later, we were having dinner with a Christian couple when the husband leaned over and said, "We feel God has told us to give you our car." His wife nodded in approval. "We've been praying about it for months," he said earnestly, "I've never felt so excited about anything in all my life. We both have Scriptures on it . . . our only fear is that you won't take it." His fear was unfounded.

He then produced the ownership papers, the transfer fee and had me sign on the dotted line. I felt such a mixture of emotions—humbled by this couple's obedience to the Lord, amazement that God was concerned about my transport and blown away by such a gift.

The car had a full length, yellow, genuine sheep-skin seat cover on the driver's side, which the couple said they felt God wanted them to leave in the car. I wanted one for the passenger side, but hadn't said anything to anyone. I was returning from my prebreakfast bimonthly run in the park one day, when I spotted something lying on the ground in front of me. It was a full length, yellow, genuine sheep-skin car seat cover! I made enquiries as to the owner, but to no avail, and came to the conclusion that when God gives you your heart's desire, He does it right down to the last detail.

What are your desires in life? If you have sought first "the Kingdom of God and His righteousness," you can expect God to take care of you, right down to the last detail. The key is to serve Him with all your heart. A young man once asked Leonard Ravenhill what was the key to success as a Christian. He just said one word— "Obedience." Bill Gothard remembered that word, took it to heart, and God entrusted him with a massive worldwide ministry. The key to success is to do whatever you do, with all your heart.

Gilbert and Sullivan wrote a song which illustrates the principle of success perfectly:

> When I was a lad I served a term, as an office boy in an attorney's firm. I cleaned the windows, and I swept the floor, and I polished up the handle on the big front

door. I polished that handle so carefully,
that now I am the ruler of the Queen's
navy.

Everyone who opened the door to the
attorney's office saw the polished handle, and it
soon brought the lad promotion. The way to
impress God is to polish up the handle of an
obedient heart of servitude. The way up is to
start low.

On 7 March 1982, I began to earnestly seek
God as to what He wanted to do with my life.
When would I begin to see a fulfillment of different prophecies given to me, and when would
God honor my deep desire to be used by Him?
One day I was reading John chapter 13, when
verse 7 jumped out at me: "What I am doing
you do not understand now, but you will know
after this." From that moment on, I had a dis-
tinct impression that God wanted me to travel
to Australia in September of that same year. So,
with this conviction, I began saying to my friends
and family, "God wants me in Australia in September." Different instances began to confirm
my confidence. The Scripture came a second
time, from a different source, "What I am doing you do not understand now."

In July of the same year, I received a call
from Australia asking if I would be willing to
come for one month in September and teach
four hundred young people from around the
world on the subject of evangelism. I said that
the maximum period of time I would leave my
family was ten days, so the man said he would

call me back in one hour. When the call came, I was told that his committee had decided to invite my whole family over. I said, "In that case I'll come for a month."

It was around that time, that I discovered the importance of the use of the Law in evangelism.

After returning from Australia, I had a dream in which I saw a shipwreck, half submerged in water, with people crying out for help around the sinking ship. I found myself running across the water towards them. I then climbed a huge rope net with the survivors. At the top of this net was a door, but the survivors were struggling to get through, because the door was small. There seemed to be confusion and congestion around the entrance. I leaned forward and submerged my hand into a wooden door which had no handle. Within the wood was a hidden handle which opened a larger door, and allowed people to get through without hindrance. Inside was a room in which survivors were eating and drinking hot soup, and were given blankets to warm themselves.

It became clear to me that the shipwreck was the world. The running on water spoke of the nature and the urgency of the Christian message. We are able to work "while it is yet day" under the supernatural power of our God. The net and the small door signified the way of salvation (Matt. 13:47, John 10:7).

How easy twentieth-century evangelism makes salvation seem—just "Say this prayer," or

"Give your heart to Jesus." Yet, we read these words in Luke 13:24: "*Strive* to enter in at the strait gate" (italics added). The word "strive" comes from a Greek word from which we derive our word "agonize." Spurgeon said of evangelism in his day:

> Possibly, much of the flimsy piety of the present day arises from the ease with which men attain to peace and joy in these evangelistic days. We would not judge modern converts, but we certainly prefer that form of spiritual exercise which leads the soul by the way of "weeping-cross," and makes it see its blackness before assuring it that it is "clean every whit." Too many think lightly of sin, and therefore think lightly of the Savior. He who had stood before his God, convicted and condemned, with the rope about his neck, is the man to weep for joy when he is pardoned, to hate the evil which has been forgiven him, and to live to the honor of the Redeemer by whose blood he has been cleansed.

Church records worldwide are full of fruitless "decisions for Christ." Others don't fall away or backslide . . . neither do they slide forward. They don't examine themselves to see "if they are in the faith." They have made their "decision," therefore conclude that they have entered through the door of salvation. Their confidence is not based upon the Word of God. But the Bible says if you are lukewarm you will be spewed out, if you are fruitless you will be cut down, if you are not gathering you are scattering, if you are not living in holiness you will not see the Lord and if you even "look back" to the world you are not fit for the Kingdom.

Multitudes of professors of faith are standing at the top of that roped net, with no Spirit-witness assurance that they have passed through the door of salvation. The modern evangelical message preaches a large, wide door of salvation, but upon close examination it is shown to be small . . . only a few of those crowds prove themselves to be soundly converted.

The concealed handle represented the Law of God. Few preachers see the Law as an evangelical tool. Scriptures such as "The Law of the Lord is perfect, converting the soul" mystify them. But those who have the courage to use the Ten Commandments to bring the knowledge of sin will find that the Law is indeed the handle that swings open the door of grace to the sinner. He who enters through that door will know true broken contrition and genuine repentance. If the noose of God's Law is pulled tight around the throat of the ungodly, if the bag is placed over his head, if he hears the trapdoor creak beneath his trembling knees, if he sees he is condemned with no way of escape . . . then, when the pardon is produced, he will receive it with unspeakable joy.

The Law produces contrition by revealing the truth of what we are in the sight of God. Look at these verses:

> For if anyone is a hearer of the word and
> not a doer, he is like a man observing his
> natural face in a mirror; for he observes
> himself, goes away, and immediately for-
> gets what kind of man he was. But he who
> looks into the perfect Law of Liberty and
> continues in it, and is not a forgetful hearer
> but a doer of the work, this one will be
> blessed in what he does. (James 1:23-25)

If we look into the mirror of the Law we see our true state. The image of what we are in truth leaves a deep impression upon our minds. We go away from the Law not forgetting what we are without the Savior's blood. The result is that we are a "doer of the work."

The only way you and I can see ourselves in truth, is to look into a mirror. Yet, a mirror can only do its job and reflect truth if there is bright light. In Scripture, the Law of God is called both a mirror, and light (James 1:23-25, 2:11-12; Prov. 6:23).

Many of today's converts aren't shown the mirror of the Law. We think that a long look at what they are in truth will be too painful for them. "All have sinned" is all they get. They are not left in the womb of conviction.

When the hearer comes under conviction that produces godly sorrow, then he appreci-ates the Savior and sups with Him in sweet communion. He passes through the door of sound conversion and "eats that which is good." He is "abundantly satisfied with the fatness of [God's] house," and "drinks of the river of

[God's] pleasures." Instead of producing a lukewarm convert, such a way of salvation produces
a "fireball" for the Kingdom of God. He becomes ignited with the flame of God's Spirit.
Another spiritual arsonist is recruited in the army
of God and thrust into battle to fight the good
fight of faith.

I met a young man once who had spent
some time in prison. He promised God that if
He allowed him to be released, he would become a Christian, but when he was released,
the man didn't keep his word. Some time later,
he was on a roof removing tree branches. Unfortunately, some builders had illegally left live
power lines hidden among the trees. As he unwittingly gripped the wire, a massive electrical
current burned its way into his body. He was
immediately knocked unconscious, and his
hands were incinerated beyond recognition and
had to be replaced with hooks.

It took some years for him to come to grips
with what had happened, working through bitterness, a divorce, drugs and pain. Finally he
found a place of genuine repentance with a total
surrender of his will to the Lord, something
evidenced by the joy in his eyes.

Sadly, the modern message of Christianity
misleads the sinner into thinking that he is at
liberty to bargain with God. It leaves the sinner
without the fear of God in his heart. What a
great deal of misery and pain would have been
averted if he had been "convinced of the Law as
a transgressor" (James 2:9), and that he could

only fling himself at the mercy of the Judge, rather than offer some sort of negotiable obedience to God. I'm sure he would be first to admit, now that he understands his unregenerate state before God, that it would be far better to enter heaven without hands than go to hell with them. Jesus said that if our best hand offends us, we should cut it off. That's a sobering testimony as to the serious nature of sin, something the ungodly cannot understand until the Law shows them sin in its true light.

Satan wants to keep that handle of the Law of God concealed. He is quite happy to see lukewarm, unrepentant "conversions." They are no threat to his kingdom, because they are still children of darkness. Most of the unregenerate have little thought of eternity until they are confronted by death. On 18 May 1993, a woman in Costa Mesa, California, saw a man steal her vehicle. When she followed him in another car, he stopped, walked back to her and said, "If you keep following me, I'll kill you." She persisted in following him, so he kept his word and shot her five times.

Fortunately, the woman lived to tell her story. As each bullet pelted her body, she cried out, "Oh my God, if I die . . . please take me to Heaven."

God's Law does more than confront a sinner with the issues of eternity. It makes them cry, "Oh my God, when I die . . . I'm going to Hell." I believe that is a great key to getting the depth of burden Spurgeon had for the lost.

Look at his own testimony to the influence of the Law upon his salvation:

> Wherever I went, the Law had a demand upon my thoughts, upon my words, upon my rising, upon my resting. What I did, and what I did not do, all came under the cognizance of the Law; and then I found that this Law so surrounded me that I was always running against it, I was always breaking it. It seemed as if I was a sinner, and nothing else but a sinner. If I opened my mouth I spoke amiss. If I sat still, there was sin in my silence. I remember that, when the Spirit of God was thus dealing with me, I used to feel myself to be a sinner even when I was in the house of God. I thought that, when I sang, I was mocking the Lord with a solemn sound upon a false tongue; and if I prayed, I feared that I was sinning in my prayers, insulting Him by uttering confessions which I did not feel, and asking for mercy with a faith that was not true at all, but only another form of unbelief. Oh yes, some of us know what it is to be given into custody of the Law!
>
> Then the Law, as interpreted by Christ, said, "Whosoever looketh on a woman to lust after her hath committed adultery with her already in his heart." The Law said, "Thou shalt not steal," and I said, "Well, I never stole anything"; but then I found that even the desire to possess what was not my own was guilt. Then the Law informed me that I was cursed unless I continued in all things

that were written in the book of the Law to
do them. So I saw that I was "shut up."

Spurgeon tasted the bitterness of the Law,
and so appreciated the sweetness of the gospel
of grace. Such experience produces a broken
spirit, one that is open to the burden of the
Lord. His Adamic nature was crucified by the
Law, on the cross of Calvary. It is fitting that
Jewish tradition says that the tablets of the Law
were similar to tombstones: "This depiction of
rectangular tablets with rounded tops resem-
bling both the shape of typical old Jewish
tombstones . . . and boundary markers" (the
Torah, p. 538, W. Gunther, Union of Hebrew
American Congregations). The function of the
Law is to give boundaries to humanity. Each of
us has transgressed those boundaries, and therefore the Law brought death to us. Martin Luther
said, "The true and proper function of the Law
is to accuse and to kill; but the function of the
Gospel is to make alive."

This is why we should never preach grace,
until we have thoroughly prepared the ground
of the heart with the Law. Martin Luther also
said:

> We can not understand or desire to hear
> the Gospel that Christ's saving work re-
> deems from sin unless we have stood un-
> der the Law. Apart from the Law, we can-
> not recognize the greatness of what Christ
> does for us and to us. The Gospel is thus
> directly related to the Law. The proclama-
> tion of the Law is the indispensable and

necessary supposition for the preaching of the Gospel. (*The Theology of Martin Luther*, p. 258)

I was once speaking to a man named Duane who would not admit that he was a sinner. When I asked him if he had lied, he said that he had. I asked what that made him. When he hesitated, I said, "A liar?" He shook his head and said, "No, I'm not a liar." I looked to his friend who was standing next to us and asked, "If Duane has told a lie, what is he?" He turned to him and said, "A sinner, man!" Duane said, "I'm not a sinner!" His friend said, "We have all broken every one of those Commandments." I reminded Duane that he had blasphemed earlier and told him to be honest with himself, which caused him to say that he was going to go to church. After a few minutes of reasoning with him about the Law, he said, "You've made a little sense today." He then smiled and said, "You do feel better after you admit the truth and be true to yourself."

It was L.O. Thompson, a respected Bible teacher of the last century who said:

The attempt to keep the Law in its spirit will lead to the revelation of self, and disclose both a disinclination and an inability; and, when this is the case, the Law becomes a schoolmaster to lead us to Christ.

SIX

Too Much at Steak

According to the "Dallas Morning News" of 11 June 1994, 68 percent of Christians in the United States don't see evangelism as being the priority of the Church. A survey carried out around the same time among the readership of the popular evangelical magazine, *Christianity Today*, found that only 1 percent of their readership had any zeal for the lost. In the May/June issue of 1994, *Charisma* magazine reported that the Barna Research Group found that 75 percent of those who professed to be born again couldn't even define the Great Commission.

Why are there so few laborers within the body of Christ? There are many who say they love God, read the Word, pray and praise God with a passion, but there are so few who have what Spurgeon referred to as a deep "tenderness." These are the ones who carry an anguish of soul for the fate of the ungodly. They break out of the comfort zone of complacency and by any means seek to save that which is lost. The love of Christ "constrains" them. The Greek word used denotes that His love arrests them, preoccupies and presses them to reach out to the lost. These are the ones of whom Jesus said there was a great and tragic lack (Matt. 9:37–38), commanding us to pray that God would give us more. They take off their jackets of condescension and go into the harvest fields. They roll up the sleeves of complacency and make bare their holy arms. They are *laborers*, ones who sweat for love of their Master and endure the heat of the day—the scorn of a godless and sinful world.

For years I couldn't discover what it was that forged these rare and hardy souls. Were these merely diamonds that sparkled more than others because of a God-given temperament? Were these people born fearless by nature and their bold and zealous witness came naturally to them, outsparkling others who lacked such a virtue? No, some of the most zealous and bold witnesses of Christ I have known have been of a quiet or even of a shy disposition.

One night in late 1994, I found the answer. A friend, Pastor Mike Smalley, and I were at the home of Winkie and Faye Pratney, deep in the heart of Texas. Winkie is a fellow New Zealander, so it was something special for us to get together for dinner—it called for steak.

Winkie went outside to put the steaks on a barbecue pit, but a few minutes later reluctantly brought them back inside when the barbecue pit ran out of propane gas. As he cooked them inside, he said something about them not being as tender as they would have been if he had cooked them on the intense heat of the barbecue pit.

After a few minutes, the entire house filled with smoke from his cooking; but it was well worth it—the steaks melted in the mouth. Besides, the fans in the house soon cleared the air.

It was when I remarked about how tender my steak was that Winkie shared his secret. He explained that the way to keep a steak tender is to "sear" it on both sides for forty seconds on a very hot hotplate. That seals the juices in the steak, then you cook it slowly until it is done.

About three o'clock the following morning, it dawned on me as to what produces the much-desired tenderhearted Christian. When a sinner comes under the intense heat of the Law of God, it has the effect of sealing within him a tender heart. This is how it happens: As the spirituality of the Law bears down upon him, it shows him the exceeding sinfulness of his heart. It reveals to him that the very core of his nature is vile, that his lust is adultery, that hatred is murder, that he is a liar, a thief, a rebel—a selfish and ungrateful sinner.

He begins to see that he has loved that which is abhorrent to his Creator. The Law shows him that even his so-called good works are tainted by a self-centered motive. This knowledge coupled with the fact that he has *greatly* angered God by transgressing His Law, and that hell is his just dessert is the "heat" that seals in the tenderness of soul.

When grace is revealed, it is embraced as a man dying of thirst embraces a water flagon. The experience of being captive to death, yet being given freely the waters of life, forever secures the virtue of unspeakable gratitude, and that makes him a laborer for life. The Law gives him understanding that in the gospel he is forgiven much, so he loves much—vertically and therefore horizontally.

Such a tenderness is difficult to cultivate in someone who already possesses knowledge of God's grace in Christ. His realization of God's goodness deprives him of the fear of wrath. Only those who can sing "and grace my fears relieved," see grace as being truly amazing.

This is why the enlightened witness of Christ is not afraid to put on the heat when speaking with sinners. He knows that when the smoke of the wrath of the Law condemns the prisoner before him, it is actually preparing his heart for a pardon that will be welcomed *because of the fear gripping the prisoner's heart*. The Christian knows that the tears that fear produces because of the Law will be wiped away by the gentle hand of God's grace, and he knows that that hand will not be fully appreciated if the Law is not allowed to do its most necessary work. It is the Law of God that exposes sin, and when sin is seen under the penetrating light of the Law, it makes grace "abound." The Greek word used in Scripture to explain this in Romans 5:20 is *hyperperisseuo* and means to "superabound."

Remember, if I were a surgeon and I knew you had a terrible disease, I would be unwise to give you a cure without first carefully explaining to you that you had the disease. However, I wouldn't merely tell you that you had the disease, I would actually let fear work for your good. I would use it to cause you to *want* to take the cure.

As I showed you x-rays, I would watch beads of sweat drip from your brow and say to myself, "Good, he's beginning to see the seriousness of his disease." The fear will not only cause you to embrace the cure, it will, when the cure is received, give you tremendous appreciation for me as your doctor for providing the cure.

A great preacher once asked a well-known actor how it was that when performers present a story they often bring the audience to tears, yet rarely do ministers move a congregation to such a degree. The actor said that they *portray fiction as if it were a reality*, while ministers of the gospel too often *portray reality as if it were fiction*.

If we really believed souls were going to hell, we would preach with overwhelming passion. Our hearts would groan in constant prayer. We would run to sinners with solemn words of warning, take hold of them and beseech for them to turn from sin. Instead, we lack any real sense of urgency. We are afraid to speak frankly with sinners about their personal sins--we are afraid to "strike" them. We think that searing them under the heat of the Law will do harm rather than good, but consider how Jesus spoke with the woman at the well in John chapter 4. He put the heat of the Law on her (verse 18) and spoke of her personal transgressions . . . and what was the result—she became an immediate *laborer* (verses 28, 29).

The loving and loyal laborer longs for sinners to come to the Savior, for without the forgiveness of sins precious souls will be damned for eternity, so he is not afraid to turn on the heat and let the smoke of an angry Sinai fill the room. He knows that in His own good time God will clear the air with the gospel. Besides, when a true and faithful witness witnesses truthfully and faithfully, he has powerful fans in heaven. That helps him see his mandate clearly. He knows that the fruit of his labor—a soul coming to biblical repentance—makes all heaven rejoice.

I received the following letter about our book called, *America, America,* which expounds the power of the Law to bring revival to the States:

> This friend of mine has always told me for the last eight years whenever the opportunity popped up, that the Law was finished with and that the Ten Commandments were basically useless. Of course, I tried to gently suggest that the knowledge of sin could not come by any way other than the Law, but this was always smothered in a sugary reference to love and grace . . . so I kept quiet.
>
> But I stuck my neck out last week and gave the book to this friend and the next day, he

handed it back to me. He was crying and shaking with emotion. He could hardly speak. He said "I've just been born again!" What really happened I think was the full impact of the power of God's Law had struck him and wounded him, showing him clearly how bad his sin really was. He was in quite a state for several days after that and kept breaking out into praise to God.

Seven Scared Sinners

Late in 1994, I arrived in Baton Rouge to do a series of meetings. I was picked up by Jeff, a Christian in his late twenties who told me of the plan he had for me to speak open-air at a "mock" funeral.

After a short sleep in my hotel I was picked up, briefed the pallbearers, the corpse and the crowd as to the do's and don'ts of an open-air, then we drove to the site of the preaching.

When we pulled into the parking lot of Wal-Mart I thought we were going to buy something there, but it was actually the location Jeff had chosen for the open-air. After about five minutes of preaching, one of the security guards approached me and said I could speak for another five minutes, then I had to stop. I was thankful for extra time and afterwards, mentioned this to the local pastor who had come with us. He smiled and said, "When you started, I said to the security guard, 'See all those people around the preacher—they go to my church and we all shop at Wal-Mart.'"

After that, we drove to an area near the local university campus and set up the funeral once again. This time Jeff had decided he would give my voice a break by preaching himself. Just as we were organizing the pallbearers, a siren shrieked behind me and I turned to see a traffic officer on a motorcycle angrily waving down a van full of teen-agers. As the van pulled to the side of the road the police officer jumped off his bike, ran to the van, opened the door and cursed the driver. He then grabbed him and violently pulled him out of his seat and thrust him against the vehicle and gave him a body-search, once again using obscenities as he did so. The scared youth didn't resist as the officer frisked him down and yelled at him.

From what I could gather, the officer had waved the van down and they had failed to stop. Some of the passengers in the van had thought the incident funny and this had caused the officer to boil over. Here was a wrath-filled slightly out-of-control "minister of God, a revenger to execute wrath upon him that does evil."

We decided that it wouldn't be wise to preach with the law so upset, so we moved right to the entrance of a bar about thirty yards across the parking lot. When Jeff preached, semidrunken teen-agers came out of the bar and mocked him. It was a replay of what I had just seen in the natural realm. These teens were refusing to listen to the Law, and they were storing up wrath that would be revealed on the day of wrath. The day would come when an angry Law would pull them from the seat of the scornful, and from that there will be no escape.

After about five minutes, the manager came out and stopped Jeff from preaching (the local church members didn't patronize his bar).

As we wandered back to the van we passed the youths the officer had stopped. I went over to the group and asked what had happened. The driver was obviously still upset and told me that he had driven through a stop sign, had his lights out and he had failed to stop when the officer first waved him down. His six friends who were with him in the van were also shaken by what had taken place. I couldn't help but sympathize a little with the driver and shared how I thought the officer had clearly lost control of himself. He agreed.

I wanted to witness to them, but felt I lacked the right approach. They were like a distressed child who had just grazed his leg, and I had arrived to put salt in the wound. I was sure if I mentioned sin, righteousness and judgment at that point of time I would be told in no uncertain and colorful terms to depart from the area, so I reluctantly told them I would see them later and walked back to our group.

As I was standing there one of the girls asked if I had witnessed to them. I said I hadn't, that I didn't know how to approach the subject and that I needed a little time to get some thoughts together.

A moment later, I walked back to them determined to say something to them about their eternal salvation even if I did get abused. Suddenly, I remembered that I had put about ten one-dollar bills in my wallet to give away at the open-air, something I often do to illustrate that faith without works is dead. When I asked how much the fine would be, the driver looked up and said, "About two hundred dollars." I took my wallet out, pulled out the handful of bills and said, "This isn't much, but I would like to give this toward the fine." As I referred to the money, I looked down at it in amazement. Right in the middle of what seemed to be a wad of bills was a ten-dollar bill visibly clear in the pile of ones making it look far more than it was. It looked like a fortune! Different ones in the group said, "Wow . . . you can't do that . . . that's really nice of you . . . you don't even know us." The driver graciously declined the money, but the offer struck a cord in their hearts. They could see that I really cared for them and the suggestion had given me license to speak to them about their salvation. I said, "I'm a preacher. Here is a gift for each of you." I then handed each of them a penny with the Ten Commandments pressed onto it and asked if they had kept the Law. When I asked if they had lied, stolen, lusted, and so on every one of them admitted they had broken the commandments.

Then I turned to the driver and asked him if he was scared when the law pulled him from his vehicle. He said he was terrified. I then said, "Tonight you transgressed civil law, but now you know that you have also transgressed the Divine Law. If civil law scared you, wait until you face God on Judgment Day . . . it is a fearful thing to fall into the hands of the Living God." I explained the gospel, asked if they had Bibles and told them to dust them down and read the Gospel of John. I then shook their hands, thanked them for listening to me and left them in the hands of a faithful Creator.

While I'd been speaking, the driver was peeling masking tape from around his ankles. He had strapped sealed plastic bags of whiskey under his socks, something the law hadn't found when he was frisked. God only knows what may have happened that night if the driver had downed the whiskey and driven home with six drunken friends in his van. The officer of the law missed that hidden offense, but God's Law won't miss a thing.

Both the civil and the Divine Law did a deep work in some young hearts that night. It was my prayer that seven "steaks" were seared to a crisp, and that some day seven fearless and faithful laborers would enter the harvest fields and gladly toil for their Master.

By the way, Winkie Pratney's talents were not confined to cooking steak. The man is not only an excellent Bible teacher and author,* but a brilliant ping-pong player, as I found out two days later. I also discovered that his style of demonstrative play was reminiscent of a woman in the latter stages of child labor. Despite the sweat, groans and screams when the man missed

---

* Winkie Pratney is the author of *Devil Take the Youngest* (Huntington House, 1985) and *Revival* (Huntington House, 1994).

a shot, I found that he was extremely talented. He played with the grace of a master. His speed, his genius, his reflexes, his dazzling shots were executed with astounding agility. Only occasionally does one get to witness such brilliance. I beat him.

SEVEN

Mine Eyes
Have Seen the Glory

In previous chapters we have established that it is very clear from Scripture that God doesn't want sinners to perish. His will is for the world to be saved. It is also clear from Scripture that we should be seeking to fulfill the Great Commission. How then can we motivate ourselves to do so? How do we break out of the comfort zone of living in our own pleasure and security and live on the cutting edge of God's perfect will? That is what we will look at in this chapter.

I wonder if you are happy with your reaction to the word "evangelism"? Does it produce a feeling of guilt or joy? Do you run to your evangelical responsibility as did Philip to the Ethiopian in Acts chapter 8, or do you run from your evangelical responsibility as did Jonah? The answer will more than likely be, "A little of both." The spirit is willing, but the flesh is weak. You could identify with me when I said in an earlier chapter I was pleased to have an empty seat next to me in a plane. Our heart wants to seek and save that which is lost, but our Adamic nature would far rather stay tucked in the bed of indifference. However, my motivation comes from the knowledge that, if I really care about the person who sits next to me, I will make every effort to witness to him.

I remember sitting next to a man in his early twenties who wasn't at all open to the things of God. He wasn't antagonistic, just apathetic. My questions received minimal response. I could have easily pacified my conscience by saying that I had done all I could to reach out to him.

As I was typing on my laptop computer, he looked at it and said, "I'm not reading what you are writing—my eyesight isn't good enough." Suddenly, I saw my opportunity and said, "This is an amazing computer. It can create huge type." I quickly typed out, "Unless you repent, you shall perish," and said, "Watch this." I put a sixty-point font in front of the Scripture, pushed a few buttons, and before the man's eyes appeared the huge wording, "UNLESS YOU RE-PENT, YOU SHALL PERISH." He was very quiet. I told him they were the words of Jesus, and that if he as much as lusted after a woman, he had committed adultery in his heart. He looked at me and soberly said, "I'm going to hell a thousand times over then." For the next few moments I had the opening to reason with him about his salvation. If we love the world enough, we will break free from every argument, reason, excuse, rationalization, defense and justification we can find for silence, given to us by the devil or by our fearful and dispassionate mind.

In the Epistle of Paul to Philemon, he tells how he continually prays for Philemon, saying that he has heard of the "love and faith" which Philemon has, both towards the Lord and towards his brethren. Then Paul says that the "sharing of your faith may become effective by the acknowledgment of every good thing which is in you in Christ Jesus" (verse 6).

The Greek word for effective means "active, operative and powerful." Isn't that what we want? We want to be active, operative and powerful in our witness for the gospel. The key to getting this is very clear. Both the love and faith Paul spoke of are not passive. Love is not dormant. If we have love for God and man, we will share our faith, because from those two fruits of the Spirit (love and faith) spring most of the other fruits. Love will produce goodness, gentleness and patience, while from faith issues joy and peace. Our love will be the gasoline to motivate us, and our joy will be the energy that keeps our battery charged.

The fact that God wants sinners to be saved is the very reason He tarries (2 Pet. 3:9), so the sooner the gospel of repentance is preached to all nations, the sooner men will repent, and the sooner Jesus Christ will return to this earth to set up His everlasting Kingdom.

The Key

In Philippians, Paul speaks of God exalting Jesus and giving Him a name which is above every name, and that "at the name of Jesus every knee should bow . . . and that every tongue should confess that Jesus Christ is Lord, to the glory of God the Father" (Phil. 2:10-11). Then he says that we should work out our salvation with "fear and trembling." How do we obtain those commanded virtues of fear and trembling— by seeing Jesus Christ as Lord. This same thought is brought out in Psalm 2:11-12. Yet, many Christians still see Jesus as portrayed in the Gospels, the man from Nazareth, limited to time and space. They still picture Him as the man who grew tired, hungry and thirsty. If that is our image of the risen Son of God, whether it be in our mind or a picture on the wall, we must rid ourselves of it because it is hindering us from growing in God.

The Apostle Paul said that we "have known Christ after the flesh, yet now henceforth know we Him no more" (2 Cor. 5:16). The word "flesh" is *sarx* and means "human nature with its frailties." Look at the Amplified Bible's rendering of the verse:

> Even though we did once estimate Christ from a human viewpoint and as a man, yet now (we have such knowledge of Him that) we know Him no longer (in terms of the flesh).

Jesus is no longer "lower than the angels."

That was purely for the "suffering of death." He is now "crowned with glory and honor." He is the Lord of Glory, all power has been given unto Him, with the glory that He had with the Father "before the world was." Isaiah saw Him in His preincarnation glory and said that he saw the Lord sitting upon a glorious throne, and that He was

> high and lifted up and His train filled the temple . . . the seraphim cried, Holy, Holy, Holy is the Lord of Hosts . . . the posts of the doors moved at the voice of Him . . . then said I, Woe is me! For I am undone! (Isa. 6:3-5)

John also saw Him in His glory and said that he saw

> the Son of Man . . . and His eyes were as a flame of fire . . . and His voice as the sound of many waters . . . and His countenance was like the sun shining in its strength. And when I saw Him, I fell at His feet as dead. (Rev. 1:13-17)

This is what the Scriptures are saying when they speak of the sharing of our faith becoming effective by the acknowledgment of every good thing which is in you in Christ Jesus. The word "acknowledgment," means to understand every good thing we have in Christ. You and I have treasure in earthen vessels. The very source of all life dwells in us. We have Christ in us, the hope of glory. In Him dwells all the fullness of the godhead bodily, and we are complete in

Him. If we could comprehend what we have in the Savior, we would never lack joy, and we would never for a minute let apathy enter our hearts. We would radiate with love for God, at what He has given us in Christ.

Paul spoke from experience when he expressed the fact of not knowing Jesus "after the flesh." We are not told what knowledge he had of Him in His flesh, but he certainly knew Jesus in His glory. The blinding light from heaven took away his eyesight, on the road to Damascus. His fleshly eyes glimpsed light inaccessible. When he wrote to the Thessalonians, his mind wasn't clouded by a false image of the Son of God, because he knew Him as the "King of Kings and the Lord of Lords, who only has immortality, dwelling in light unapproachable." He wrote that the Thessalonians shouldn't be troubled because

> the Lord Jesus shall be revealed from Heaven with His mighty angels, in flaming fire taking vengeance on them that know not God, and that obey not the gospel of our Lord Jesus Christ: who shall be punished with everlasting destruction from the presence of the Lord, and from the glory of His power. (2 Thess. 1:8-9)

As we see Jesus Christ as the Lord of Glory, we will not only work out our salvation with "fear and trembling," but the fear of God in us will begin to work for the salvation of those around us who are the heirs of eternal damnation.

This same vengeance with fire is spoken of by the prophet Isaiah in chapter 66:

> For behold, the Lord will come with fire, and with His chariots like a whirlwind, to render His anger with fury, and His rebuke with flames of fire. For by fire and by His sword will the Lord plead with all flesh: and those slain by the sword shall be many. (verses 15–16)

A Christian friend once told me how his daughter jumped out of bed, and with a radiant face told how she had dreamed of the coming of the Lord. She said how she had heard the trumpet sounding and had seen Him in His glory, flames were leaping from housetops and those who were inside were fleeing in terror. But this little girl woke up radiant, because she was forgiven, she had nothing to fear. She was one of those who will "love His appearing." The Scriptures tell us that it "does not yet appear what we shall be, but we know that when He shall appear we shall be like Him for we shall see Him as He is" (1 John 3:2). The second the trumpet sounds, in one "twinkling of an eye," we shall be transformed into a body not subject to the terror that the ungodly will feel. We shall have boldness on that great day, but for those still in their sins, that day will be a day of unspeakable terror! Paul says, "It is a fearful thing to fall into the hands of the living God . . . wherefore knowing the terror of the Lord we persuade men."

Each of us should be able to say with the hymn writer:

> Mine eyes have seen the glory of the com-
> ing of the Lord; He is trampling out the
> vintage where the grapes of wrath are
> stored; he has loosed the fateful lightning
> of His terrible swift sword, His Truth is
> marching on.

What Must Our Sins Be Like?

The prophet Isaiah tells us of our unregenerate state before God by saying that "we are all
as an unclean thing, and all our righteousnesses
are as filthy rags; and we all do fade as a leaf,
and our iniquities, like the wind, have taken us
away" (Isa. 64:6). Note carefully that it is not
our sins that are as filthy rags in His sight, but
our *righteousnesses*. If that is the case, what must
our sins be like in the perception of our Holy
Creator? If that which is "highly esteemed"
among men is an abomination in the sight of
God, what must that look like which is detest-
able among men?

The Day of Vengeance is in God's heart, He
will "tread them in His anger," and "trample
them in fury." You and I only see the tiny tip of
the bitterly cold iceberg of sin with the work-
ings of the Mafia, prostitution, strip clubs, filthy
movies, child pornography, drug pushing, cor-
ruption, greed, lust, torture, hatred, cursing,
blasphemy and crime. In fact, by the time you
take to finish this chapter, in the United States
alone, more than seven people will have been

either strangled, stabbed or shot to death. If the given statistics hold true there will also have been more than 50 robberies, 110 cars stolen and 360 burglaries! Each year in the United States over 4 million women are victims of domestic violence, and in the same time period 550,000 women are raped.

We see only the tip, but the Bible says, "The eye of the Lord is in every place, beholding the evil and the good." Proverbs 15:26 tells us that even the thoughts of the ungodly are an abomination to the Lord. Jeremiah says, "The heart is deceitful above all things, and desperately wicked." If we don't embark upon desperate evangelism, using every means God has given us to convince, induce, persuade and compel them to come in, God will convince them on that day when He comes "with ten thousands of His saints, to execute judgment on all, and to convince all that are ungodly." But then it will be too late!

David said in Psalms, "Their inward part is very wickedness," while Paul speaks of sin being "exceedingly sinful." He then gives God's view of humanity:

> Their throat is an open sepulcher; with their tongues they have used deceit; the poison of asps is under their lips: whose mouth is full of cursing and bitterness: their feet are swift to shed blood: destruction and misery are in their ways: and the way of peace have they not known: there is no fear of God before their eyes. (Rom. 3:13-18)

Passion for Vengeance

In Arizona in 1981, two men offered to help a lady in distress. She had locked herself out of her car and they very kindly helped her open the car window. Now there's a point in favor of the goodness of man. How could this woman repay the men? They suggested a six-pack of beer. She went into the store, bought the beer, but when she came back they abducted her in her own car. Both the men raped the young woman, then tied her hands and feet and went to her apartment. They ransacked it, stole her valuables and found to their delight, that she had a bank card with eight thousand dollars in savings. Unfortunately for them, they were only able to withdraw $250 per day using the card, so it would take some time to get the whole eight thousand. They both concluded that they couldn't let her live. They waited until dark, then took her, still bound hand and foot, up a mountain. They raped her again, then threw her off a cliff. She landed half way down, and they could hear by her groans that she wasn't dead, so they threw her off twice more. Despite this, she was still alive so they hit her head with rocks until she was unconscious, then buried her alive.

If you are anything like me, you will grapple with tears, anger, shame and a cry for justice for those men. This passion for just vengeance upon those wicked men is there despite our sinful nature. If the deeds of those men seem abominable even to us, the sinful offspring of

Adam, how evil must they seem to a holy, perfect and just Creator.

With all this wickedness leaving us "found wanting" in the scales of God's justice, humanity in blind foolishness says within his heart, "God has forgotten: He hides His face; He will never see it" (Ps. 10:11). But as surely as God is faithful to all His promises of blessing upon the obedient, so is He faithful to His promise of cursing upon the disobedient. He will fulfill His Word which He has magnified above His name. The Scriptures warn sinners that in accordance with their hardness and impenitent hearts they are treasuring up for themselves wrath:

> In the day of wrath and revelation of the righteous judgment of God, who will render to each one according to his deeds . . . to those who are self-seeking and do not obey the truth, but obey unrighteousness—indignation and wrath, tribulation and anguish, on every soul of man who does evil. (Rom. 2:5-9)

In 2 Peter, we see that God made an example of the angels that sinned, casting them into hell, delivering them into chains of darkness to be reserved for judgment. The same is the case with the Noahic flood and Sodom and Gomorrah—they were condemned, "making them an example for those that should live ungodly." Amidst the filth of Sodom, where dwelt men who were "wicked and sinners before the Lord exceedingly," was righteous Lot. This man "vexed" (anguished, pained) his "righteous soul from day to day with their unlawful deeds." Are we anguished by what we see in the world? Are we jealous for the honor of our God? Are we grieved beyond words to see His mercy despised and His holy name blasphemed? At the same time do we cringe in fear for the ungodly who walk after the flesh in the lust of uncleanness, full of presumption and self-will, with no fear of God before their eyes?

Jeremiah had this same conflict when he cried,

> Oh, that my head were waters, and mine eyes a fountain of tears, that I might weep day and night for ... my people. Oh that ... I might leave my people and go from them! For they are all adulterers, an assembly of treacherous men. (Jer. 9:1-2)

Many Christians aren't "vexed," because they either don't "know" the terror of the Lord, therefore they don't seek to "persuade men," or they are living in a monastery without walls, losing contact with the world. Life consists of Saturday night fellowship, Sunday services, Wednesday Bible study and a few other social activities. They are living in a Christian comfort zone, where little contact is made with the ungodly world.

Directly after the command to work out our salvation with fear and trembling (Phil. 2:12), we are told:

> It is God who works in you both to will and to do of His good pleasure. Do all things

[including God's will—to seek the lost] without murmurings and disputings, that you may be blameless and harmless, the sons of God, without rebuke, in the midst of a crooked and perverse nation, among whom you shine as lights in the world, [then we are told what on earth are we supposed to be doing] holding forth the Word of life, that I may rejoice in the Day of Christ. (verses 13–16)

We have been commissioned to, "Go into all the world" (Mark 16:15). "I do not pray that you should take them out of the world." (John 17:15). With these Scriptures in mind, how many publicans and harlots are our friends that we might reach them for Christ, or is our "world" made up of Christians? Are we light among light, salt among salt? Do we seek God for men in fervent prayer, then seek men for God in zealous evangelism? Paul charged Timothy to "preach the Word in season and out of season," and the previous verse tells us why: "the Lord Jesus Christ, who shall judge the living and the dead at His appearing and His Kingdom." The awe of that day should cause an urgency to burn in our hearts.

EIGHT

Necessity Is Laid Upon Me

It is obvious throughout Scripture that God speaks to humanity through dreams. He spoke in this way to Joseph, Daniel and numbers of others through that medium. In fact, it says in Joel chapter 2 that this will be one of the signs of the last days. I don't know if some I have had are God speaking to me, or just dreams, but I do know that some have attributed to my zeal for the lost.

I remember having a dream that I was standing at an outdoor restaurant. People were happily eating and drinking, when I distracted them by saying,

> Excuse me, may I have your attention for a moment. Last week I came to this place and I was fearful to tell you something. This week I want to tell you what I should have then . . . unless you repent, you will perish!

Some carried on eating, others looked angered, while others looked down under conviction.

Even though many Christians would rather it not be so, this is the simple message of the gospel. Jesus told his listeners that if they didn't repent, they would perish. This is the message of John 3:16. The reason Jesus died, was so that those who believe "should not perish, but have everlasting life." God gave His only begotten Son, so that sinners wouldn't perish in hell.

Like Paul, we must reason of "sin, righteousness and judgment." Yet, this has been a glaring omission from the message of twentieth-century evangelism. We have failed to warn our hearers to flee from the wrath to come. Another gospel has been preached, and another harvest has been reaped, leaving the church impregnated with many false converts.

John Wesley knew what it was to "save with fear." He said, "I desire to have both Heaven and Hell in my eye." In other words, he wasn't happy merely to get his ticket to heaven without reaching out, by all means, to save those from the fire of the wrath of God. He caught a glimpse of the vision of John's words in the Book of Revelation when he said that the heavens,

> departed as a scroll when it is rolled together; and every mountain and island were moved out of their places. And the kings of the earth, and the great men, and the rich men, and the chief captains, and the mighty

men, and every slave, and every free man,
hid themselves in the dens and in the rocks
of the mountains, and said to the mountains and rocks, fall on us and hide us from
the face of Him that sits on the throne and
from the wrath of the Lamb; for the great
day of His wrath is come, and who shall be
able to stand? (Rev. 6:14-17)

The word "wrath" means that God has a
violent passion for justice—our "righteous Lord
loves righteousness." If, when we see injustice,
something in us cries out against it, how much
more does God crave eternal justice! The reason God anointed Jesus, was because He "loved
righteousness and hated iniquity." Look at these
verses that give us insight into God's character:

Let not the wise man glory in his wisdom,
let not the mighty man glory in his might;
nor let the rich man glory in his riches. But
let him who glories, glory in this, that he
understands and knows Me, that I am the
Lord, exercising lovingkindness, justice and
righteousness in the earth. For in these
things I delight, says the Lord. (Jer. 9:23-
24)

If God gave us the wisdom of Solomon, we
would have to give Him glory for the gift. If He
gave us the strength of Samson, we would have
to give Him glory for the endowment. If God
gifted us with riches, we couldn't boast of them,
for they came by the goodness of God.

Our glorying should be confined to the fact,
not that we "understand God," for no one can

understand the incredible mind of the Lord, but that we understand that:

One, He is the Lord. He is the Supreme Authority in the universe, that from Him and through Him and to Him are all things. Every man will give an account of every idle word to Him.

And, two, we understand, that He not only exercises lovingkindness, justice and righteousness in the earth, but that He *delights* in these things. This is seen in no better place than on the cross of Calvary. This is where there was a meeting of lovingkindness and justice. This is where righteousness and peace kissed each other. This is why Paul said, "God forbid that I should glory, except in the cross of our Lord Jesus Christ." It is in the cross that we see the fearful justice of our Divine Creator, as His wrath-filled fist came down upon the Lamb of God. It is on the same cross we see infinite lovingkindness displayed, as we understand the substitutionary sacrifice, that we might live eternally.

Many years ago, when I was a teen-ager at school, we had a music teacher who lacked a lot in the area of discipline. The poor man was also slightly deaf and consequently, when he was playing the piano, chaos broke loose behind him. During one of these lessons, I noticed a friend two rows from the front, trying to shake off a classmate who had grabbed his leg and was pulling him under the bench. I crawled under the benches in front of me and took hold of the culprit's leg, when I felt someone grab my leg. Without looking behind me, I used my free leg to kick off this leg-puller with a firm grip. It was then that I glanced behind me and saw to my horror that it was the principal, who had come into the room to see what all the noise was about!

The three of us were sent to his office. Before we were given our punishment, we had a ten-minute wait. When the principal finally arrived, he gave us two painful swats in the area designed for the purpose, but I must say with all solemnity, that the fear we had while waiting for the cane was just about as bad as the pain which came from the cane when it came.

With all the conviction I can muster, I can say without any qualms of conscience, that I would far rather receive ten thousand swats a day for a hundred years, by the right hand of the most robust football player, than be in my sins on Judgment Day . . . it is a fearful thing to fall into the hands of the living God.

When God gave His Law "so terrible was the sight, that Moses said, 'I exceedingly fear and quake!' " How fearful will it be when the fury-filled God of vengeance comes to punish those who have deliberately transgressed that Law?

Keith Green, wrote these sobering words:

> O God our Lord: Who you gonna throw in the lake of fire, O God our Lord? Who you gonna throw when the flames get higher, O God our Lord? The devil and the man with the dark desire, O God our Lord!

Do we care enough to pray? Do we care enough to preach . . . to warn, to witness? God's justice will be so thorough that every sinner will be "ground to powder" by the stone of the wrath of God. They will drink the wine of His wrath. The psalmist cried, "Horror has taken hold on me because of the wicked who forsake Your Law." J. Oswald Sanders pleaded in prayer, "Give us souls, lest we die!" Jeremiah cried, "My bowels, my bowels! I am pained at my very heart, my heart makes a noise in me, I cannot hold my peace, because you have heard. Oh my soul, the sound of the trumpet, the alarm of war" (Jer. 4:19). Listen to the "sowing in tears" spirit behind these words of C. H. Spurgeon:

> When I've shot and spent all my gospel bullets and have none left and little effect seems to be made upon my hearers, I then get in the gun and shoot myself at them.

In other words, when he had preached the truth of God's Word, his burden was such that he opened his own heart and simply implored sinners to come to the Savior. In reference to his passionate preaching to the lost, the Apostle Paul cried, "Necessity is laid upon me!" He was saying a "continual, intense distress" was laid upon him. Joseph Alleine, a Puritan of the sixteenth century, wrote a book called *Alarm to the Unconverted*, which greatly influenced C. H. Spurgeon and George Whitefield. In it, his zeal for the unconverted is very evident. Listen to his heart as he prepares to plead with the sinner:

But from whence shall I fetch my argument? With what shall I win them? Oh, that I could tell! I would write to them in tears, I would weep out every argument, I would empty my veins for ink, I would petition them on my knees. Oh how thankful I would be if they would be prevailed with to repent and turn? (1671; reprint, Puritan Paperbacks, Carlisle, Pa.: Banner of Truth Trust, 1978)

Look at his burden—"I would empty my veins for ink." How many of us would empty a pen of ink to warn a loved one or a friend to get right with God? Are we prepared to let God "lay necessity" upon us? Do we want the communication of our faith to become effectual?

Forget the Kids

Most, nowadays, are familiar with air travel. It is standard practice in most countries to have airline attendants stand in the aisle and draw your attention to the exits in the plane. Then, in a calm voice they say something like, "If an oxygen mask should appear in front of you, place it over your mouth and nose. If you have children, attend to yourself first." Why do the airlines say that? Don't they care for children?

The answer is simply because they know that if a parent has six young children, and he tries to put a mask over their faces, by the time he reaches the last child, he himself will probably be gasping for breath. They understand that the parent will be most effective if he attends to himself first.

In John 8:31-32, we see how a Christian can become effective:

> Then Jesus said to those Jews who believed in Him, "If you abide in My word, you are My disciples indeed. And you shall know the truth, and the truth shall make you free."

There we have the biblical definition of a "disciple"—he is one who has disciplined himself to continue in the Word of Christ, and this results in freedom. This is a freedom from sin, death and judgment, and freedom to reach out to others and be effective in our witness to them. Sadly, many Christians are ineffective evangelically because they are still gasping for air—they have not attended to themselves first.

Stan's Dog

Many years ago, I had a friend who was quite a character. My friend Stan placed a marijuana plant in his father's greenhouse, and his father unwittingly watered it, thrilled that at last his wayward son had come to his senses and taken an interest in botany. Stan also had a dog he called Circles. It was so named because it would walk forward two or three steps, and then do a complete circle, then another two or three steps forward, then another complete circle. It wasn't a trick, it was just the way the dog got around. I don't know if the canine is still alive, because he would cross the street the same way. Apparently, as a young pup it had been locked in a small shed for great lengths of time. It went around in circles, seeking a way out, and when it came out, it couldn't stop.

Many Christians are just like Circles. They continue to go around in circles—pew to altar to pew to altar to pew—wearing out both the pastor and the carpet. If you are such a person, pay close attention, because I am going to share with you the biblical key to get you out of the shed, and onto the straight and narrow path you are supposed to be walking.

Here is the key:

> Blessed is the man who walks not in the counsel of the ungodly, nor stands in the path of sinners, nor sits in the seat of the scornful; but his delight is in the Law of the Lord, and in His Law he meditates day and night. He shall be like a tree planted by the rivers of water, that brings forth its fruit in its season, whose leaf also shall not wither; and whatever he does shall prosper. (Ps. 1:1-3)

If we fulfill the stated requirements, the Bible promises we will be tall and strong, like a tree planted by rivers of water. Our roots will be deep, and we will therefore bring forth fruit in season (love, joy, peace, patience, goodness, gentleness, faith, meekness and temperance); and whatsoever we do, will prosper—our vocation, our marriage, our evangelical endeavors.

I have saved myself hours in counselling time, by simply asking the problem-laden, defeated, joyless, circles "Christian" one question before he unloads his burdens on me. This is the question: "Do you read God's Word every day, without fail?" The usual answer is "sometimes" or "sort of" or "most days." The truth is they are not continuing in the Word of Christ, they don't know the truth and they are not free. They are not meditating on the Word "day and night," so they are therefore not like a tree planted by water. Their roots are shallow, so when the winds of adversity blow, they topple over and need to seek the pastor to prop them up. Neither does their fruit remain. They lose their peace and joy and begin to wither at the first sign of adversity, and whatever they do does not prosper.

These poor souls look at joyful Christians and say, "It's alright for them to be happy; they never have any problems." Yet, that isn't true. Ask around, you will find that all Christians have trials, but the ones who keep their joy are the ones who fulfill the requirements of Psalm 1—their fruit remains. They stand tall and strong during the storms, because their roots go deep into God's Word. They are not blown away by "every wind of doctrine."

God gave a similar promise to Joshua. If he kept the Law, if he would "meditate" on it "day and night," God said he would be "prosperous" and reaffirmed it with "and then you shall have good success" (Josh. 1:8). So for your own sake and for the sake of those around you who are still in their sins, discipline yourself daily to the Word. Put your Bible before your belly. Say to yourself, "No Bible, no breakfast; no read, no feed." The biblical priority is to put your spirit before your body (1 Thess. 5:12).

Jesus said to His disciples, "I have food to eat that you know not of," and that "man shall not live by bread alone, but by every word of God." Job summed up the necessity for feeding on the Word:

> I have not departed from the command-
> ment of His lips; I have treasured the words
> of His mouth *more than my necessary food*
> [italics added]. (Job 23:12)

Imagine walking along a street and seeing a child stumbling along, his stomach protruding from malnutrition, his eyes bulging and his cheeks drawn in. You stop him and say, "Hey kid, are you O.K.? Are you eating your food?" He replies, "Sometimes, but I don't like eating vegetables." You tell him sternly, "If you don't eat you will die! I don't care whether you enjoy eating vegetables or not, eat them regularly!"

It makes no difference whether the Christian enjoys the Word as he reads, or whether he finds it somewhat dry, it still benefits him. He is to "daily deny himself," follow Jesus, and "desire the sincere milk of the Word."

Two drunks walked along a wharf one dark night, climbed into a small boat and determined to row to the other side of the lake. The first drunk rowed for about one-and-a-half hours, sweat pouring from his brow, until he finally collapsed. The second drunk took the oars and rowed for three hours, until he collapsed, exhausted. When they awoke at sunrise, they found to their amazement that they had made only one mistake, they were still tied to the wharf!

Sadly, many professing Christians are still tied to the wharf of self-will. To them, the burden of Christ is not "easy and light," but one of labor and sorrow, and the Christian life is one of struggle, sweat and misery. Their problem is a lack of discipline. They are bone lazy, or worse, strangers to genuine repentance. If they would feed daily on the Word, they would find that it produces faith (Rom. 10:17), and faith is what Satan hates. Faith moves mountains. I have seen the most miserable of Christians rise up in victory, once they grasped the Psalm 1 principle of feeding daily on the Scriptures. The Bible is a supernatural book. When its pages are read with faith in the heart, that faith produces more faith, and from confidence issues joy, and from joy issues a "continual feast" for the soul so that he will live in victory over life's circumstances.

NINE

Fired for Succeeding

In August of 1992, *Reader's Digest* published an article called "How 'average' people excel." It related how "fast-trackers," people who succeed in school, often fizzle. Their main problem is that they are driven by their own inflated ego, and they set goals too high for themselves. They, more than anybody, understand how clever they are, so they are never happy with playing second fiddle to anyone. In other words, their pride is their own downfall. The article, written from a purely secular point of view, had some very relevant thoughts that we may apply to the Kingdom of God. Here are the keys found by a corporate consultant, who interviewed over 190 men and women that one would consider to be "ordinary" individuals who had achieved secular success:

1. Learn self-discipline. This is the key to being successful as a Christian. Of course, we don't measure success in dollars as the world does, we measure it in terms of our lives being

pleasing to God. Self-discipline means discipline of self, and this in turn means discipline to Jesus. It means that we read the Word daily, and obey what it says. Self-discipline means self-denial. It means listening to the voice of our conscience and the voice of the Spirit. Consider Jesus in this respect. His ministry was a complete denial of self, from the temptation in the wilderness to Calvary itself. He denied His own will and disciplined Himself to the will of the Father for the sake of the Kingdom of God.

2. Bring out the best in people. There is nothing more pathetic than a selfish person. The Christian has crucified selfishness, and now lives to love his neighbor as much as he loves himself. The dividends are rich. He who loves others will be loved himself, and he who brings out the best in others will bring out the best in himself. Jesus lived and died for others.

3. Build a knowledge base. Think of Jesus as He sat as a twelve-year-old at the feet of those who could give Him understanding of the Scriptures. He grew in grace and in the knowledge of the things of the Kingdom of God. We are commanded, "giving all diligence, and to your faith virtue, and to virtue knowledge." To do so is to enrich the life of the Christian.

4. Develop special skills. Our skills are not in the natural realm. We seek skills that will save sinners from everlasting damnation. We long to be skillful by rightly dividing the Word of truth, a skillful workman that needs not be ashamed. We develop a dexterity that we might

be sensitive to the voice of the Spirit, so that we might speak a word in season to those who are weary.

5. Keep promises. A Christian would rather die than not keep his word. He "swears to his own hurt" (Ps. 15:4). If he says he will do something, he will do it if it is at all possible. In doing so, he is merely following after righteousness and simply doing what is upright.

6. Bounce back from defeat. I have had many failures. I have begun writing books that I have abandoned. I have printed tracts that I have thrown into the trash. I have floundered while witnessing. I have wasted money on projects that have failed. I have preached dry sermons, prayed pathetic prayers and made just about every blunder one can make. When our ministry first started back in 1974, we published a Christian paper called "Living Waters." On the back I ran a large advertisement headed with the words "Problems? Just call this number. You don't have to say a word . . . just listen." The number was for a local dial-a-sermon, and I thought it would be a blessing to those who found themselves needing comfort. Unfortunately, I forgot to include the area code and some poor woman in another part of the country began getting calls with heavy breathing on the line. People with problems called her and they didn't say a word. They just listened.

I heard once about a Christian who approached a young man who was selling *Playboy* magazines and asked what he was going to do

on Judgment Day, when God held him account-
able for every sale. The man gave his life to the
Savior. The incident was a fresh encouragement
to be bold.

I was reading a newspaper in an airport in
Hawaii, when a stranger walked by and asked,
"Any good news?" I said, "Yes. If you repent of
your sins and give your life to Jesus Christ, you
will pass from death into life." Do you know
what happened? Nothing . . . the guy was a
Christian!

I could write a book solely on flops, wash
outs, mess ups, botches, duds, bungles and failures, but who hasn't blown something in his
life? Those who blunder the least are usually
those who attempt the least. Steven Pile, the
head of the Not Terribly Good Club of Great
Britain, was recently forced to resign from his
position when a book he wrote called *The Book
of Heroic Failures* became a best-seller. He
couldn't even succeed in his position as presi-
dent.

Gathering Sticks

A young man once asked if I thought he
should go to a mission school. I asked him how
many people he witnessed to each day and found
that he actually spoke to six or seven people
daily about the things of God. His business was
carpet-cleaning, and that gave him a personal
contact with sinners from various walks of life.
We looked at his future as a student. He would
go to a Christian training school and spend six

months with no one but Christians. Then he would go out and do mission work . . . if he still had a mind to. Charles Spurgeon said, "Be careful when you are picking up sticks, that your fire doesn't go out."

If you don't witness and you feel you need training, go to a Bible school where you know they have a burden for the lost, so that you will end up with more zeal than when you went in. Or better still, get into a lifestyle where you rub shoulders with the world. I gained what knowledge I have through godly teaching and a number of years of open-air preaching. The latter was a case of sink or swim.

A friend of mine was a very proficient "garbiologist." He collected the garbage for a local company. He said it wasn't too difficult, because you just picked it up as you went along. The same applies with evangelism. You will pick it up as you go along. It really isn't hard to witness, if you know what you want to achieve. It isn't the big deal the devil makes you think it is. Just find someone who is open to Christian things, take them through God's Law, then the cross, repentance, then faith. There's the skeleton. It's just a matter of putting the flesh on as you go. As you make witnessing a regular thing, it will come to you more naturally. In fact, it will come to you supernaturally, because you will have the help of God. The best way to learn to swim is to get into the water, then once you figure out that it isn't that difficult, you will get back into the water with less fear.

For the Thinking Mind

I was sitting at a Long Beach airport feeling quite happy with myself. Good music was being played on the sound system, two people were tapping their feet and one was whistling along with the music. I had been upgraded to first class (because of frequent flying), and was actually looking forward to boarding the plane. It means you get into the plane before the masses, and that takes the stress out of flying.

I had put Ten Commandment pennies into the change slots of the telephones, and had placed Christian literature on a number of the seats, and what's more, I had avoided the dreaded cleaning lady. More than once I have filled an airport with literature, and found to my dismay that the cleaning lady was cleaning up after me by putting all the tracts in the trash.

If you want to break out of your serenity zone, go to an airport. Where else in today's busy world can you find people sitting, doing nothing? We have one tract which is excellent for airports. It is called the "Book Mark" and has plenty of "get-away time." It doesn't look at all like a Christian tract, and gives you plenty of time to get away. Its heading boosts the ego by saying, "INTELLIGENCE TEST . . . for the thinking mind." Below the heading are eight brain-teasers. Number seven asks a question about a man who had broken the Ten Commandments. When he made it to the gates of heaven, he found that God was "just," and had to, by His very nature, punish sin. How could God let him into heaven and still be just? On side two, it gives all the answers, including an explanation of how God did it through the cross.

At larger city airports, you will find tens of thousands of people. What's more, many of them are from all around the world. This is your opportunity to begin an international evangelistic ministry. At a Dallas airport for example, one airline has about thirty gates. Have someone drop you at gate one and pick you up an hour later at gate thirty. During that hour, you walk through, dropping these boredom breakers on the empty seats as you go. I have done it hundreds of times, and never once have I been reprimanded, because what I am doing is totally permissible by law as a constitutional right according to a recent court case:

> The high court said airport authorities may prohibit repeated solicitation of money by political and religious groups. But the court also ruled that such organizations have a First Amendment right to distribute their literature in airports. (*Wall Street Journal,* June 1992)

Maybe you have a library full of good Christian books. Take a handful, and leave one on the seat you've been sitting on. Just make sure you don't do this in an airport that is in a big mess, because the cleaning lady will come along and do her thing.

Are you grateful for Calvary? Then show God your gratitude. Give Him the "widow's mite" of your witness. The incident of the widow giving her last two coins to God shows us that only the gift that costs counts. God knows that for you to slip a tract onto a seat may be equivalent, on a courage level, to some other Christian standing up and preaching. But you can do it. Don't listen to your fears. Say, "If God is for me, nothing can be against me. I can do all things through Christ who strengthens me." Then do it. Civil law is still on our side—you'll not be thrown to the lions. Let the devil eat dust.

Catching Fan

I am not a big fan of fishing. In fact, I don't like fishing, I like catching. But to catch, you have to fish. I love to see people come to the Savior, but that only comes if I continually fish for men and women.

I now want to show you a wonderful witnessing tool. For me to do this, you will need a blank piece of paper. So put this book down for a minute and go and get a piece of paper . . . it will be well worth your while. If you haven't got access to one, you will find a blank page in the back of this book. This will be ideal for what I want to show you—you will have to trim the edge straight though (if you make a jagged edge while ripping it out).

Now do exactly what I tell you (this may seem complex, but it is very simple). Fold the paper, from the top, down one third. You should now have a square piece in your hand. Fold the left top corner into the middle and crease it down. Fold the right corner down and crease it, as though you are making a paper plane. You should now have something that looks like a house with a pointed roof. Continue making a plane by folding the paper in half. Crease it down the center. You should now have something that looks like a paper plane before you fold the wings down.

Now turn the point of the plane towards the ground, with the shorter edge to your left. Starting at the top left side, place your thumbs and forefingers a little more than a third across to the right, and carefully tear downwards in a straight line, until you have torn the piece off altogether. Place the torn piece on a table where it won't blow away. Then rip off the same width as the first piece vertically (rip it as straight as you can). Place this piece with the other, then put the remaining (long) piece on the table, away from the other two strips. Now open the two pieces, and carefully make them into letters. You will find two L's, and the other pieces of paper will form the letters E and H. When you put them all together, you will have the word HELL, (if you have been careful to do exactly as I say). The remaining long piece, when opened, will form a perfect cross.

Here is the story that goes with this: A Christian was once talking to an atheist and a churchgoer. The atheist said he didn't believe in heaven, hell, the cross, or in God (as you are telling this story, you begin folding the paper). The Christian warned him that he would have to face

God whether he believed in Him or not. The church-goer said he believed everything the Bible said, but he hadn't repented as yet. While the Christian pleaded with them both, a truck came around the corner, up onto the sidewalk and killed the three of them.

As they stood before the Judgment Throne of God, the ex-atheist looked down and saw a piece of paper in the Christian's hand. He said, "That's a ticket to get into heaven, give it to me!" The Christian said, "I'll tell you what I will do. I will give a third of the ticket to each of you" (this is where you tear off the two strips, and place the longer one away from them.) Then you pick up the two pieces and say, "So they took their tickets, and gave them to God. The Lord said, 'Let's see where the tickets say you are to go.'" As you open them, they spell the word HELL.

Then you say, "The Christian walked up to the Throne and gave his one third of the ticket to God, who said, 'The only way to get in, is the way of the cross,'" and you open the third piece, revealing the cross.

This is an excellent way to conclude a time of witnessing to someone, as it sums up visually what you have been saying. If they die in their sins, and face the Law, God will give them eternal justice and they will end up in hell. But if they shelter in the cross, He will give them mercy, and everlasting life.

Leave It All

A number of years ago, a movie was made called, *The Fourth Wise Man*. It was a fictitious story, centered at the time of Christ, about a Magi who was hindered from travelling with the three wise men who took their gifts to Jesus. The man epitomized the spirit of the Law. When he and his servant came across a stricken stranger, they bathed his wounds, and when they had to leave, the Magi said to his servant, "Leave him with sufficient bread and water." When the servant protested, "There is hardly any left," the Magi said, "Leave all of it then."

The act so spoke to my heart. The servant was saying that there was barely enough to keep them alive, and was no doubt hoping his master would say not to leave any, or at least to leave the minimum. But this man did to others as he would have them do to him, fulfilling the Law and the prophets. Such acts of kindness don't come naturally to us, but with the help of God, we can express our love for the lost in that spirit.

If you have the Spirit of Christ, you will have what the Scriptures call "the wisdom that is from above." This is how the Amplified Bible renders James 3:17:

> The wisdom from above is first of all pure (undefiled); then it is peace-loving, courteous (considerate, gentle). It is willing to yield to reason, full of compassion and good fruits; it is wholehearted and straight-forward, impartial and unfeigned—free from doubts, wavering and insincerity.

Don't be concerned that you aren't "gifted" as a speaker when it comes to reaching the lost. The Bible says of Moses, he "was learned in all the wisdom of the Egyptians, and was mighty in words, and deeds" (Acts 7:22), yet God didn't use him to deliver Israel until forty years later. Instead, it took all that time of tending sheep to produce a meekness of character different from that which he had in Egypt. The Bible says, "the meek will He guide in judgment: and the meek will He teach His way" (Ps. 25:8-9). The wisdom that Moses gained from Egypt was not a wisdom from above. When he saw injustice, he took the law into his own hands and committed murder (Acts 7:24). God doesn't need the wisdom or the mighty words and deeds of this world. He merely desires a pure, humble, peace-loving, compassionate soul to use as a mouthpiece for the gospel. He wants us to be a lighthouse of His love. The moment we receive the Spirit of Christ, we receive the gift of those virtues. We don't need to tend sheep for forty years when we have the character of the Good Shepherd manifesting through us.

If you want to see souls saved, witness whenever and wherever you can. If you sow, you will reap in due season. In being a true and faithful witness, you will make sure you are in the perfect will of God. It is His Word that commands us to preach the Word "in season and out of season." When I go out to witness and can't find someone to speak to, I sit down and pray that God will bring someone to me. I remember approaching three females once, and as I got closer, I noticed they were speaking in Spanish, so I sat down and prayed for someone to come to me, knowing that I was in God's will. Sure enough, within sixty seconds, two young men sat right next to me. I overheard one of them say that they were stuck there until 9:00 A.M., so I knew I had at least thirty minutes to speak to them.

One of them came under conviction when I spoke of his personal sins and he glanced at his watch twice. I told him that he had until 9:00 A.M., so there was no need to worry about the time, and that it was guilt that was making him feel uncomfortable. That made him smile. Sometimes people don't realize why they react the way they do. I prayed with them both individually, and for God to heal an injured arm of one of the men, and they seemed very appreciative.

In an earlier chapter, I mentioned how I use I.Q. tracts when witnessing. These little cards make it so much easier for me. Probably the most difficult thing about witnessing for most of us is swinging from a conversation about something like the weather to the subject of the things of God. At that point, our fear of rejection runs wild. These tracts make the swing from the natural to the spiritual as smooth as butter. People do the test on side one, then go straight into the questions about God, almost always without offense. The best way to show you their potential, is to have you do the tests yourself:

TEST YOUR I.Q.
READ this sentence:

> **FINISHED FILES ARE THE RE-SULTS OF YEARS OF SCIEN-TIFIC STUDY COMBINED WITH THE EXPERIENCE OF YEARS.**

Now count aloud the F's in the box. Count them only ONCE; **do not look back and count them again.** If you think you are right, look on the back.

There are six; if you found three, you are normal. Usually seven out of ten people get three F's. If you found three, go back and check again. We have had people write to us and say, "There aren't six F's," and have had to send the card back with the F's circled. If you can't find them, write to us and we will circle the three "of's" you missed.

TEST YOUR I.Q.
Read OUT LOUD the wording in the three triangles:

Now take a look at the back and see if you are correct:

If you said, "Paris in the spring, Bird in the hand and Once in a lifetime," you got three wrong, try again. The word "the" and "a" are repeated. It's obvious, once you see it.

Here is the third test:

Add these numbers:

One thousand plus forty. Now add another thousand. Add ten. A thousand more. Add forty. Now add ten more. What is your total?

You probably think the answer is 4,000. We mistakenly think 3,090 plus 10 is 4,000, when 3,090 plus 10 is actually 3,100.

Each of these tracts gives the answer on side two, then there are six questions about the things of God:

Here is another I.Q. test; answer yes or no OUT LOUD:

1. Is there a God?
2. Does God care about right and wrong?
3. Are God's standards the same as ours?
4. Will God punish sin?
5. Is there a hell?
6. Do you avoid hell by living a good life?

The answers are: (1) yes, (2) yes, (3) no, (4) yes, (5) yes, and (6) no. You can't afford to be wrong; find out the truth—ask God to forgive your sins, then trust Jesus Christ, who took your punishment by dying on the cross for you. Read the Bible daily and obey what you read . . . God will never let you down.

How to Use the Card

As I have said, the most difficult thing about witnessing, is bringing up the subject of the things of God. The card does that for you, inoffensively. Another difficulty, is knowing what to say. The card will help guide you through the gospel. Often people are self-confident and proud—the card will almost always humble them—don't leave home without it.

Often you don't know if the person you are speaking to is trusting in grace or in self-righteousness—this card will find that out for you within two minutes of meeting him. In fact, it will also tell you his intimate beliefs about God, sin, hell and judgment.

Since I was converted in 1972, I have given out fifty to sixty thousand tracts (not to the same person) and have experimented in ways to get them into the hands of the unsaved. I've found that there is an effective and inoffensive way to get strangers to take a tract. Keep the cards in your wallet or purse, then as you are getting one out (you will have their attention as you are giving them something out of your wallet—so it is of value), ask, "Did you get one of these?" This question has a twofold effect. It stimulates curiosity, as well as making them feel that they are missing out on something (which they are).

As they take it, they will usually ask, "One of what?" Smile and say, "It's an I.Q. test." Most people will also smile when they hear this (something to do with the human ego); it is so refreshing to have someone smile when given a tract. Many will try it straight away. As they read it, build a bridge by gently pointing out the object. If they fail the test, be sensitive that they may feel embarrassed when you point out their error. Take the opportunity to relate to them, saying that the majority fail it. Then say, "Now try the other side."

Don't worry if the person passes the test on side one; just say, "You did well . . . now try the other side, it's far more important."

So far you have had time to get to know the person (especially if they failed the test). Now comes the next benefit of this card. The majority of those who look at the second side, begin to "play the game" and actually do what the card says; they read OUT LOUD the answers to the six questions on side two—1) Is there a God? They say, "Yes" or "No." 2) Does God care about right and wrong?, and so on.

It is some consolation to know that in recent polls 96 percent of Americans believe in God; 82 percent believe in an afterlife, and approximately 60 percent believe in hell. So, few are offended by these questions.

When they answer out loud, you have an excellent opportunity to ask why they think such a thing, and thus get to witness to them.

When someone says they think God doesn't care about right and wrong, most can be reasoned with by appealing to civil law. Almost everyone thinks murderers should be punished (even if they can't agree on its form). Then say that if man, with all his evils cares about right and wrong, how much more will his Creator!

With this little card, in two or three minutes, you can build a bridge with a stranger, break down his confidence in his own judgments (eight out of ten times), find out his crucial beliefs, find out whether he is trusting in self-righteousness or grace, as well as witness to him, inoffensively. When he answers the six questions, you can say, "You did well . . . you got four out of six correct. One that you slipped up on was number three, when you said that God's standards are the same as ours. The Bible says, 'His way is perfect'—'Who shall ascend the Hill of the Lord; He who has clean hands and a pure heart,' 'Blessed are the pure in heart' " or other similar passages.

Learn the spirituality of the Law. Study what the Commandments mean in the light of New Testament revelation. So digest the Ten Commandments, that you can go through them one by one, opening up each one to show that God requires truth in the inward parts.

Then, once you have clearly presented the Law, say, "And the other one you slipped up on was you said we avoid hell by living a good life. The Bible tells us, 'It is not by works of righteousness that He saved us, but according to His mercy' (Titus 3:5)."

After you have thoroughly brought the knowledge of what sin is, using the Law of God, uphold the cross in all its glory. Other advantages of these cards is their low cost (three dollars for a hundred), they are easy to distribute and are extremely convenient (you can easily carry twenty in your wallet or purse). Keep a stack with you because you will often be asked for more.

Don't feel as though you have to lead every

person you witness to in a sinner's prayer. I pray with most people I witness to. If they are trembling, and saying something like, "What then should I do?" then I pray with them for salvation. If you lead someone in a prayer of repentance, and they haven't yet gained godly sorrow through conviction of the Holy Spirit, you may deliver them, but it will be a stillborn or a premature birth. If by chance they are genuine in their commitment, then you will have to incubate them and the odds are, like most premature babies that begin to grow, they will be sickly and weak. It is best to let them form in the womb of conviction, then in the timing of God, they will be born again, and merely need to be fed the sincere milk of the Word. When fruit is ripe for the picking, it should fall into your hand, and when someone is ready for the Savior, you shouldn't have to prize them away from the tree of the world. In fact, if someone is ready for salvation, you probably won't have to lead them in prayer, because the prayer will come from his own heart.

I once heard a respected pastor speak of being in an airport awaiting departure. He had trouble finding a seat, and after moving several times, found himself sitting next to a man whose wife had just died. Tears welled in the man's eyes as he spoke of the meaninglessness of life. The pastor was able to witness to the man about God's love for him. He even prayed with him, but he didn't lead him in a "decision." His reason was that when a person is in such a broken state, you can get them to pray anything. He gave him literature, put him in contact with a pastor in his area, but he left the man's salvation in the hands of the Lord. That takes faith in God. It takes courage because the inclination in most of us is to get a decision for Jesus and cut another notch into our evangelical belt.

Did your parents ever make you kiss and hug your brother or sister to "make up" after a fight? Did it come from your heart, or did you grit your teeth and make up for fear of wrath if you didn't? A sinner's repentant prayer should come from his own heart, and not because he feels compelled to because of wrath, but because he has sinned against the God of heaven. It should come to his heart as the words came to the heart of the prodigal son (Luke 15:18). He should have "godly" sorrow, because he has transgressed the Law, and "repentance towards God," because he has "sinned against Heaven."

By the way, sometimes when you are witnessing, you will meet people who think they know everything. One way to have a little fun and advance the cause of the gospel at the same time is to ask them if you may ask them seven questions. To see the power of these little "humblers," put this book down and have someone *verbally* ask you these questions and write down your answers (if you just read them yourself, you will fail to see their impact):

1. How many of each animal did Moses take into the ark?

2. What is the name of the raised print that deaf people use?

3. Is it possible to end a sentence with the word "the"?

4. Spell the word "shop." What do you do when you come to a green light?

5. It is noon. You look at the clock. The big hand is on three, the small hand on five. What time is it?

6. Spell the word "silk." What do cows drink?

7. Listen carefully: You are the driver of a train. There are 30 people on board. At the first stop 10 people get off. At the next stop 5 people get on. Now for the question, what is the name of the train driver?

Answers to questions:

1. None, it was Noah.
2. Deaf people don't use raised print.
3. The question is an example of one.
4. Go.
5. Noon.
6. Water.
7. *You* are the driver of a train.

TEN

Stirred to a Frenzy

As I flew over the city of Des Moines, Iowa, I could see snow on the ground, something fascinating for someone coming directly from the southern Californian climate. As soon as I arrived at Teen Challenge in the city of Colfax, I sent a cold fax to Sue, saying it was a cool thirty-one degrees. Freezing though it was, I was ushered into a warm guest room. In fact, my room was so warm I woke in the night with an intense thirst. Fortunately, I had opened the first of the double windows and placed a bottle of sparkling, natural flavored mineral water in the cooler air for such a time as this.

I reached out in the blackness of the night and unscrewed the lid. Suddenly, I found myself beneath a fountain of cool mineral water as it burst from the bottle. The cold weather, plus the movement of my hand picking up the bottle, had been enough to stir the contents to a frenzy. It was quite an outburst.

God sometimes puts His children out in the cold for a reason. Moses had great desire to be a deliverer, but God put him on the shelf for forty years. He knows that the pressure of desire is building within the vessel of those that love Him. All it will take is for Him to shake the Christian, just a little, then release the cap of that which is hindering the living waters from flowing out into this dark world.

Never be discouraged by the thought that God has put you on the shelf for no reason. If you love God and are called according to His purposes, then whatever is happening to you is happening for your good (Rom. 8:28). He is working in you to will and do of His good pleasure.

I once spoke at a church where the pastor was very zealous for the lost. A year later, I returned to the area to find out that the man's wife had run off with a lesbian who had been fellowshipping at a local church. She had also taken most of the house contents as well as his charge cards, running them to the limit and leaving him fifteen thousand dollars in debt. As if that wasn't enough, a few members of his church didn't like the fact that this had happened and began murmuring to a point where he was forced to resign from his office. He found himself out in the cold.

It seemed God had put him on the shelf, but within one year, God had taken him in His hand and released him back into ministry. He was part of a new work in another state. The time will come when God will fully release the restraint, when many will be showered in times of refreshing from the presence of the Lord, because of the result of the pressure that dear brother went through. God only shakes the Christian for the furtherance of His purposes. The world suffers in vain, we suffer for our own profit and for the profit of the world—if we are "exercised" by whatever experience God takes us through. When the devil seeks to sour our hearts by putting bitterness in our minds, faith will not let that happen. The man who trusts in God says, "Though He slay me, yet will I praise Him."

I once finished ministering and, longing for a place to rest, could see only one chair at the back of the church. It was blocking the entrance of the recording booth and had a sign draped over it saying, Do not enter. Of course no one in his right mind would sit on a chair with a sign on it.

As I stood up after about five minutes of resting my weary body in the chair, a young man (very apologetically) said, "You have the words 'Do not enter' written on your back." The sign had been written in eyeliner and was now embedded in black on my white shirt.

One fiery dart that Satan loves to discharge at the Christian is the dart of bitterness. The pastor who found himself stripped of everything, still has on the armor of God. No one could take away his shield of faith from him—he could stand, and having done all, stand. However, it has been pointed out that there is no provision for the back of the Christian, so the enemy needs to know that he will find the shield of faith in the way of a direct frontal attack and a "Do not enter" notice, if he tries to enter subtly through some back door. God left Joseph simmering in a prison for thirteen years. He was bound in chains, and it seemed he would have had every right to become bitter towards Potifer and his sex-starved wife, his brothers, as well as towards God, but faith wouldn't let that happen. Bitterness didn't find an entry into his heart, even through the rear door.

Joseph's life has great lessons for the Christian. Not only is it a hidden "type" of the life of Jesus, but it carries within it instruction, direction and encouragement.

I have often wondered if Joseph did the right thing in telling his brothers of his dreams. Even his father was upset on hearing of them. Human nature is such an unstable thing, it doesn't take much to uncover jealousy within the heart. Knowing my own heart, I am careful to whom I boast of some of the good things God does for me. I would hate to cause another Christian to stumble in any way because of unwise words on my part. But Joseph insisted on telling his brothers, and it stirred a unified murderous spirit that almost cost him his life.

Sometimes we have no choice. When we come to a knowledge of salvation, we cannot but speak that which we have seen and heard. To our friends and family, we sound as though we have had but idle dreams. They, like the brothers of Joseph become stirred by the god of this world, and because of the gospel, direct hatred at us. God however, moves in the life of the Christian, as He did in the life of Joseph. We find ourselves being lifted to places of responsibility. He found himself as a trusted servant in the household of Potifer. Things were going well for Joseph, when one lusty lady enters the scene. This was a sinner's dream, contrived in the cunning minds of hell's residents. She whispered, "Stolen water is sweet, and bread eaten in secret is pleasant." She personifies the seductions of sin as it whispers in the mind of the Christian. Don't listen to her voice! Cry out to God to uncover her wickedness. Plead for Him to make her voice odious to your ears. Ask the Father to make the sweet taste of lust bitter to your pallet. Resist sin, and be steadfast in the faith. Say with Joseph, to the seductive voice of lust, "How could I do this thing and sin against God!"

Look at the spirit that motivated Potifer's wife. When Joseph didn't yield, she showed how much she really cared, unleashing her acidic heart when he rejected her advances. It was the same spirit that used Judas for its insidious purpose. So Joseph found himself in prison because he wanted to do the right thing. In a world that loves sin, those who stand for righteousness will suffer. In doing so, they may receive a frown from the world, but they have the smile of God. Blessed are those who are persecuted for righteousness' sake, for theirs is the Kingdom of heaven.

If you are faithful in small things, God will trust you with bigger things. Late in 1992, I received a call from a pastor in Texas, in whose church I was to speak. He had been trying to get me into a large Bible school called Christ For The Nations, with whom I had had no previous contact. They were booked up with speakers for the next two years, and it didn't seem very hopeful. So, I called them and found out who was in charge. The top man, Dennis Lindsey was on vacation and his mother whose name was Freda was in charge. I found their fax number and began writing a letter to fax to them, saying how important the teaching was that I was wanting to share.

I had written "Dear Freda," and three paragraphs when the phone rang. A voice said: "Hello, I'm calling from Israel. I have just heard your 'Hell's Best Kept Secret' teaching on tape. My name is Shira, my mother and father's names are Gordon and Freda Lindsey, and my mother runs Christ For The Nations in Dallas, Texas. This teaching is so vital, I am going to send my mother a fax and ask her to have you speak there."

I couldn't believe it. I had the fax on the screen in front of me, with her mother's name already written. God's timing was perfect for me, and His timing will be perfect for you . . . in His time.

Fighting Prejudice

A friend once called and asked if I would be interested in getting into a business selling high-tech personal alarms. He sent me the literature, an alarm and tapes showing the company's credibility. I was convinced that it could be a way for my eldest son to make a living, but to make sure, I decided to test the product myself. I put on some dressy clothes, a striking tie, and began to beat the sidewalk of our local boulevard.

The experience was horrible. Almost everyone, as soon as they saw I was selling a product, took that as a license to treat me as if I was a conman. If I was buying something, then I deserved courtesy, but because I was selling, there was immediate impatience, intolerance and prejudice. Almost every manager to whom I spoke had the presupposition that I was out to hoodwink him. The experience reminded me of the fact the most of us are very prejudice. We judge people on how they look, the clothes they wear, the style of their hair and even by the car they drive. Even as Christians, we can be prejudiced. I heard of a pastor of a large church, who sat down with his staff and said, "We are going to watch a video I disagree with," as he switched on our "Hell's Best Kept Secret" teaching. After the screening, he said, "I would just like to say, that I agree with everything on that video." His limited and second-hand knowledge had shaped prejudice in his heart. Once he understood the basis of the teaching, he was able to accept it as legitimate.

Unregenerate contemporary humanity is bent on prejudice when it comes to the things of God. Their limited knowledge leaves them with a prejudicial attitude. They have been programmed into thinking that we are fanatical, religious fundamentalists. However, if they only knew what we have in Christ, if they could only have the light of understanding about the issues of eternity, they would listen with baited breath. This is why our first contact with an unsaved person is so important. We can't let them justify their prejudice. While we speak to them on a natural level, they should be feeling the warmth of a genuine sincere heart. Then, when they find that we are Christians, they should be saying within their minds, "This person is different." These first few minutes are a time to establish basics in both speaking and listening.

The following are listed by a group called Media Management as the ten most annoying mistakes made while listening. For business, it can mean a loss of money, but in the Kingdom of God, it can mean that we are not as good a witness as we could be, so we should strive not to fall into these errors:

1. Lack of eye contact.
2. Disagreeing with everything said.
3. Holding side conversations.
4. Correcting grammar or word choices.
5. Answering before the question is finished.
6. Not responding.
7. Bad breath or sitting too close.

8. Completing speaker's sentences.
9. Coughing or clearing throat.
10. Interrupting.

Most of us don't listen very carefully. Take for instance the camera crew who took a camera to the streets and asked a number of people what they would do if they found that their best friend was a "homo sapian." A number of people said, they "would never speak to him again!"

Notice also that the first thing on the list is eye contact. Of all the people on the earth who should be able to look the world in the eye, it is Christians, because we are speaking the gospel truth. There is no ulterior motive—we are not selling anything, all we are "after," is the person's eternal well-being.

I'm a regular guest on an interesting talk-back radio program called "Religion on the Line." The two-hour show has a Catholic priest, a Protestant minister, and a Rabbi as guests each week.

Once Sue and I arrived at the studio we were let in by the security guard. As we signed the necessary forms, he asked, "How was church today?" I told him it was good, and asked if he was a Christian. He said he was one once but had fallen away from his faith. I told him that the thing to get him back to the faith was a look at the Ten Commandments. I asked him if he had lied. He had, so I said, "What does that make you?" He hedged, by saying, "Story-teller." I smiled and said, "Come on . . . what does that

make you?" He said, "A liar." He had also stolen and was therefore a thief, but when I asked
him if he had ever broken the Seventh Commandment by lusting after a woman, he said he
had never done it. I didn't believe him, so when
his eyes looked down in conviction, I put my
hand on his to get back his eye contact and
said, "Now be honest." His eyes then sparkled,
and he said, "I'm gay." It was then that I lost
eye contact. *I was holding his hand!* Sometimes
things don't go the way you planned.

The other annoyances on the Media Management list are reasonably obvious, except
number seven. Ask any preacher who has had
to endure a time of counselling at an altar call,
and he will confirm that when Adam fell, so did
his breath. I have had to counsel people while
standing sideways as though I wanted them to
speak into my ear, when I was really hiding my
nose. I have even rubbed my nose while listening to people in an effort to protect the delicate
instrument. It should be the sinner of whom it
is written "Their throat is an open sepulcher,"
not the Christian. People should not think of
Lazarus when the Christian opens his mouth. I
remember sitting in a plane listening to a man
give his life story. His breath made an open
sepulcher seem like the fragile scent of a rose.
I kept eyeing the emergency door, and fully
expected the other passengers in the plane to
have pulled down the oxygen masks to get relief. This man was a walking insect repellant.
When he bit into an apple, I thought there would

be a burst of applause from the captain, the crew and all those on board. In my heart I was saying, "Thank you Lord, O thank you Lord."

Hi Folks, Give Me Your Money

It was early in the new year of 1993, and the mall in which Sue and I strolled was comparatively quiet after the busy Christmas rush. So when we entered a store, a young man said, "Hi folks, how are you doing?" The cynical thought entered my mind, "You really mean—'Hi folks, I couldn't care less how you're doing. All I want from you is your money.'" Then he said, "If you have any questions, feel free to ask them."

I waited for about ten seconds, strolled across to the counter and said, "I have a question. What is the meaning of life?" He didn't hesitate for a second, but said, "The meaning of life is to live it to the fullest." I said, "That's what you *do* with life, but what is its purpose?" He was stumped, so I said, "If you are not a Christian, life is utterly futile, because death will take your life from you, no matter how full it is." He agreed saying, "That's true, death is the only sure thing in this life." God has given all of us a will to live. The most dense of human beings knows that life is better than death, and I know from Scripture that all of us are under the power of the fear of death, until we come to the Savior (Heb. 2:15). The human heart longs for immortality, or at least longevity.

Robert A. Chesebrough, the Brooklyn chemist who invented Vaseline, believed he had the answer for those who wanted to live a long life. He said the answer was to swallow one spoonful of Vaseline each day. He died at the age of ninety-six in 1933 . . . probably choked.

I told the man in the store that the only two things that are sure in life, are death and Judgment Day, and gave him a penny with the Ten Commandments stamped onto it, saying that that was the standard of judgment, that we've all broken the Law, and that we all need the Savior. He agreed, and we parted in good spirits. That three-minute conversation put the "eternal" into a transitory stroll through the mall. I didn't go out especially to witness, I was just ready for any opportunity if it came along. My mind was programmed to stay out of my comfort zone.

The Found "Link"

A friend, who works as an animal control officer, came by my home to visit. As we were talking, he said he had an animal in the back of his truck that would be an excellent evangelical tool for me. My mind rushed through a jungle of animals in anticipation. Was it a snake to illustrate the subtleties of the devil? Was it an elephant to portray the weight of God's Law? I hoped it would be a monkey, something I have wanted for years. Sue says we have had three children, and that should keep me happy, but a monkey would have so much potential for open-air preaching. I would dress him in blue shorts with suspenders, a red shirt, white socks and sneakers. I would train him to give out tracts to the crowd, springboarding off him into Darwin's theory of evolution. I would name the chimp Link. I could say that I finally found what evolution called the "missing link."

As Steve opened up the side of his truck, suddenly I saw the animal he had in mind. It was a skunk! I jumped back, then immediately ran inside to get Sue. Perhaps if I said I wanted a skunk, she would lean more easily towards a chimp. I used a similar principle to get our first bird. I went into a pet store and suggested we buy a big fat white rabbit. She said, "What do you want that for!" So I said, "How about a little bird then?" and she said, "Alright, just a little bird." If you want a dog, first propose getting a horse, a horse—an elephant.

When Sue came out to the truck with me, I saw something I hadn't seen before. The skunk was stuffed. It looked alive, but it was as dead as dead could be. I felt a little stupid, but quickly picked it up and ran to show my daughter Rachel, who was on the phone. She thought it was real and screamed. In fact, she almost lifted the roof off the house. It seemed the deceased skunk could raise as much—if not more—of a stink dead than it did alive.

When Jesus lay in the tomb, He was dead. Death had laid its ice-cold hand upon His body. His skin was drained of color. His heart sat like a cold rock within His breast. His cold fingers lay still and stiff. Suddenly, deep within the heart of the Son of God came a beat . . . one beat whose implications resounded blessed hope throughout the whole earth. Another heartbeat followed, then another. Within seconds, color began to return to the flesh of the Messiah. His stiffened fingers began to move, His chest raised as He breathed air into His still lungs. Life broke the steel bands of death from the body of the Son of the Living God. Just as four words from the mouth of the Creator had caused light to flood the universe in the beginning, so, in this new beginning, light had flooded the dark tomb. It was not possible that death could hold Him!

Death, the stinking skunk that it was, is now dead, in fact, it is more than dead. Its very guts were torn from its body. Now, death is but a stuffed beast, and like Steve's skunk, can only scare those who lack the understanding that it is lifeless:

> Death is swallowed up in victory. O Death, where is your sting? O Hades, where is your victory? The sting of death is sin, and the strength of sin is the Law. (1 Cor. 15:54-55)

The wages of sin is death. Jesus appeased the Law in full on the cross when He "redeemed us from the curse of the Law, being made a curse for us." He satisfied the court of eternal justice, now the prison doors have been swung open wide for those held captive by Satan to do his will.

I was preaching at a fabricated funeral in Colorado. As I stood on a soapbox in front of six pallbearers and a (living) corpse that was covered by a white sheet, about 150 people stood and listened to the good news that death had been conquered in Christ. Suddenly, the crowd began laughing. I turned around and saw a very small child sitting on the corpse! While most who watched the funeral stood wide-eyed in the face of death, this toddler rested himself on the corpse, as though it were nothing but another of life's everyday experiences.

Those who fully understand the victory wrought on the cross, and the triumph of the Resurrection, refuse to fear death. They, like the child, see no threat. It is but an empty hand grenade, a defused bomb, a stuffed skunk. It is no threat to them, nor does it have any power over them. Death is under their feet through faith in Jesus Christ. It is but a dark door with a golden handle, that opens to the pure and brilliant light of eternal joy.

How tragic that the world doesn't know what we have found in Jesus Christ. We must work while it is day, and use our energies while we have them. God forbid that life should pass us by while we are building a Kingdom that can be moved. If the Lord tarries, we will find that old age will hinder us from doing exploits for God that are a breeze to the young. It is fine for the elderly to be young at heart, but the heart needs a body that can move. We need to pray that God makes us bold and fearless before we become bald and hairless. May He use our eyes to see the harvest while we can still see. May He

use our ears to hear the cries of the lost while
we can still hear. May He use our mouths while
we can still speak, our hands to reach out to the
unsaved, and our feet to carry to them the gospel
of peace.

The Bungie Cord

On one of the many times I passed through
an airport, I placed my briefcase and my bag
carrier on the x-ray machine, and was left with
the rubber "bungie" in my hand. So, I hooked
it over the steel bar on the carrier and went to
walk through the security doorway. As I did so,
I thought, "I hope that bungie hook doesn't
catch on something as it goes over the conveyer
belt." Sure enough, one glance showed me that
the bungie had caught on something, and was
stretched to its fullest capacity, stopping my case
from moving through the x-ray machine.

We can find a similar thing happening when
we come before God and say, "Search me of
God, and try me." When we put our case on the
x-ray machine of the searching eye of God, we
hook a bungie cord onto some secret sin. That
small sin could be our downfall. It may be a
deep-rooted unforgiveness towards parents. It
may be a love for something or someone, when
we know in our heart that such an inordinate
affection is immoral. We must, for the sake of
the gospel, unhook the cords of restraint and
abandon ourselves to God, not only because He
may have something better for us, but for
conscience's sake, and for the sake of the lost.

Many years ago, there was a movie called *Alfie*. It was the story about a good-looking gentleman who committed adultery with a middle-aged mom. He took advantage of the woman's depressed state and she became pregnant. Obviously, this complicated things, so they both agreed that the pregnancy should be terminated. After the abortion, the man insisted that the doctor show him the fetus. He came out from behind the screen with a horrified expression on his face and said, "It's a child!"

Every sin has some terrible repercussion, either in this life or in the life to come. This knowledge should keep you and me from the sinful pleasures that the world offers. Just as the man who instigates an abortion knowing it is a human life he is destroying is more guilty than he who is ignorant, so the Christian who gives himself to sin, sins in light and therefore is more guilty than the ignorant.

I can recall speaking to a man who totally rejected the Bible as having any worth. Besides that, he was sure that it was not possible that any human being could understand its message. He told me that monks had been studying it for hundreds of years, and not even their learned minds could interpret its words, so how could any man off the street understand the Scriptures? When I informed him that that was why he needed the Holy Spirit to lead him into all truth, he said he didn't believe in the Holy Spirit—"just in God."

As he puffed on his cigarette, he spoke of the sins of other Christians, used God's name in vain and told me that he went to church every week and confessed his sins. Then he said that all we need to do was follow the Ten Commandments, something it was obvious he didn't do. If we do "follow" the Law, it acts as a schoolmaster to lead us to Christ.

So, we went through the Law. He admitted that he had stolen ("just a comic" when he was young). He also acknowledged that he had lied (when he was young), but when I said that God considered lust to be the same as adultery, he recoiled. It was one sin he didn't confine to his youth. That touched a raw nerve. He said there is nothing wrong with lust . . . if "you don't dwell on it for too long." Now here is a strange thing. Lust is O.K. for a time, but the duration of period in which a man lusts turns it from purity to iniquity. The god he believed in was obviously not the God of the Bible. When I asked him what his name was, he told me it was Art, and suddenly it made sense. Here was another case of idolatry. His was another god, "graven by art and man's device."

Of course the Bible is a hard book to understand, until we are born of the Spirit. There are many passages in Scripture that don't make any sense at all to the unregenerate. If a sinner is seeking salvation, he may read the words of Jesus to the rich young ruler and end up in error:

> If you want to be perfect, go, sell what you
> have and give to the poor, and you shall
> have treasure in Heaven; and come, follow
> Me. (Matt. 19:21)

It seems clear—straight from the mouth of
the Master. To get to heaven all a man has to
do is sell what he has, give to the poor and then
"follow" Jesus. But then he turns to Ephesians
2:8-9 and reads:

> For by grace you have been saved through
> faith, and that not of yourselves, it is the
> gift of God, not of works, lest anyone should
> boast.

Those who are not born of the Spirit, and
don't understand the difference between Law
and grace, will understandably end up in the
state of confusion. The Chinese language sounds
strange to me. Yet, a four-year-old Chinese child
can understand it completely. Why? Because he
has been born into a Chinese family. The Chinese language is not darkness but light to him.
The language of Scripture will be nothing but
babble to those who are not born into the family of God. The natural man receives not the
things of the Spirit of God, neither can he know
them, they are foolishness to him, because they
are spiritually understood. He must be born of
the Spirit, into the family of God, to understand spiritual things.

Nobody Understands

A pastor friend of mine often takes teams to
rock concerts to give out tracts. He designs lit-

erature with the group's lyrics on the front. He then uses them as a springboard to answer the questions on the inside, then through the Law into grace. In April of 1993, he took a team to a Guns n' Roses concert, and handed out a tract with the lyrics from their hit "Dead Horse" on the front: "Nobody understands, quite why we're here, we're searching for answers that never appear."

He and his team walked the long lines of people boldly saying what the authorities at the concert were saying: "No alcohol, no drugs, no cans or bottles." As they did so, they gave out tracts.

When the pastor arrived home, he found a message on his answering machine. It was from Mr. Rose, and he was blooming mad. He introduced himself and then said:

> How dare you blankity-blanks give out your blankity-blank, blankity-blank at my blankity-blank concert. You have a blankity-blank nerve using my blankity-blank lyrics on your blankity-blank! Click!

Had he dropped his four-letter words, his message would have been about five seconds long.

The next day, the pastor found another message on his machine. This one was much longer, and it was from a young lady at the concert who had come to the Lord directly as a result of the tract. Her voice was soft and sincere as she spoke words of appreciation, that they cared enough to break away from their own comfort zone to go to the concert to reach out to the lost. I'm sure the pastor would gladly face the thorny rebuke of ten thousand roses, if it meant the salvation of even a single soul.

In 1993, I was invited to speak at Yale University. I was excited because of the opportunity to speak at a university with such a reputation, and, I learned, a godly heritage. I found out that 78 percent of the first graduates went into the ministry, that famous Christians of the last century, such as David Brainard and Jonathan Edwards, who preached America's most famous sermon, "Sinners in the Hands of an Angry God" were students there.

When we arrived, a zealous young man named Brian showed me around. He showed me the poster advertising homosexual activities on the door of the chaplain of the divinity school. He pointed out that of the 240 students in the "divinity" school only about 10 percent were Christians. It was so sad to see a place which had old drinking fountains with "If any man thirst, let him come to me and drink," engraven into them, and doors with Bible verses cut into the wood, so given to the devil. Posters advertised student orgies in the "Brainard underground," and others announced homosexual activities on campus, all with the chaplain's blessing. Divinity professors put themselves above Holy Scripture as they sat in cynical judgment over it, rather than letting Scripture judge them.

As we looked at the heritage of the university, I noticed a party of children, all around eleven years old, standing on the grounds of the university. They seemed to be a tour party who were having a break from the tour, so I approached them with one of our I.Q. test tracts, then did some sleight of hand. Before I knew it, I was surrounded by eighty children, and preached to them for ten to fifteen minutes. When one of them recited most of the Ten Commandments by memory, I gave him a few dollars as a reward. This seemed to get the attention of the rest, who not only listened, but almost fought over tracts when I finished speaking to them.

That afternoon, I set up a soapbox in front of about twenty students who were lazing on the grass, studying. Most of them didn't appreciate my presence one bit, and a few began heckling with conviction enough to enlarge the crowd to about eighty students.

I was thrilled, because I had heard that, even though 96 percent of mainstream America believes in God, this is down to 65 percent in ivy league universities. When an atheist denied God's existence, I asked him if he had ever seen a building which didn't have a builder, a painting without a painter, a car without a maker. Had he ever seen anything that was made which didn't have a maker. It is such simple reasoning, but as these thoughts entered his ears, it was as though a light came on in his eyes. He seemed to listen after that.

The next day, Brian took me into the heart of New York by train, and we spoke at Washington Square in Greenwich Village. The place reminded me of the square in which I had spoken for many years, but there were a lot more people and a lot more drugs. When we preached, we had much opposition. One woman fumed because I said that abortion was wrong. When I asked her if her baby was born a month premature, if she would cut its throat herself if she didn't want it, she said she would. I guess she is at least consistent. That's exactly what the doctor does while it's in the womb (it is legal in some states of the United States up to nine months).

As we were leaving the square, Brian said, "We will preach on the train going back through the Bronx." I remember thinking, *"You've got to be kidding! Are you nuts?* The Bronx has a murderous reputation at the best of times. If people were offended when preached to in the open, from which they could leave, how much more angered would they be if they couldn't get out?" He couldn't see my thoughts, so I said, "Let's do it!"

The train went through the Bronx, and it was packed to capacity. Brian broke the ice this time. He made his way into the middle of the carriage of ninety people, introduced himself and began preaching. Not one soul objected. They just sat there and listened. I felt so proud of this new friend of mine as he boldly warned them of Judgment Day, and preached the cross of Calvary. In fact, I became so encouraged, I tapped him on the shoulder and whispered, "I want to preach." It showed me how you and I can give courage to others by paving the way. We both preached, gave out over three hundred tracts, and felt so excited, we could hardly sleep that night.

When I told a friend in California that we had preached on the trains in New York, he widened his eyes and said, *"What about the conductor?"* I smiled and said, "Oh, we didn't have any music . . . we just went straight into the preaching."

ELEVEN

We Are Not Ignorant of His Devices

Since the time of Christ, there has been continual opposition to the gospel of salvation. Jesus said, "You shall be hated of all men for My sake," while Isaiah said, "he that departs from evil makes himself a prey"—not only game for those who love darkness and hate the light, but for the anti-Christ spirit which rules the world (Eph. 6:12, 2 Cor. 4:4). From the time of Nero, when Christians were set on fire as torches to illuminate the darkness of his gardens, to the present day, Satan has sought to come against the gospel with every means possible.

During the many years I have had the privilege of preaching outdoors, I have not seen as hostile a spirit as I have seen recently. As the world throws itself blindly into sin, the more it will hate righteousness. When I first started preaching back in 1974, there was a semblance of opposition, but as time has passed, the antagonism has become more intense. I remember open-air preaching once, when a woman began accusing me of the "judge not least you be judged" thing. Suddenly, the whole crowd of about two hundred people, in one great wave of anti-Christ spirit, became a vast lynching mob. The incident gave me some understanding of what Stephen came up against when his listeners were offended by his words. Humanity seethes with hatred for the truth, and all it takes is a little stirring for that enmity to boil over. Many a Christian would have followed in the bloody steps of Stephen had not civil law restrained the ungodly.

Some weeks after the "judge not" crowd, an angry young man, who looked like the type who came out of the tombs, picked up a large wooden cross, which a Christian had leaned up against my preaching-ladder, and used it as a hammer to smash the ladder into a thousand pieces in a fit of demonic rage. I stood back and thanked God that the ladder was bearing the reproach and not me.

A few days later, a well-dressed plump woman in her early thirties, came out of the crowd, yelled at me in the most obscene language, slapped my face, then punched me in the mouth. A few weeks after that a heavy dude, who said that he had "been sent into the local square to stop the preaching," made me want to do what Jesus said, and flee into another city when persecuted. I repented of fear, but the next time he was in the crowd, he had a can of gas in his hands. I remember thinking as he listened to me preach, "I want to be on fire for God, but not like this!" More repentance.

The following day he stood in front of me again, and in a fit of rage, screamed out obscenities as I preached. This time I was not at all fearful. There were two reasons for this. The first was because God was with me, and the second (unbeknown to the man), was because two policemen were standing directly behind him. Suddenly, he stopped the obscenities and began to, in a deep powerful voice yell, "Get out of my way! Get out of my way! Get out of my way!" He bellowed this about twenty times then the police made their move. It took them more than twenty minutes to arrest him and put him in the squad car. I watched fear come on the faces of the non-Christians, who could hear the animal screams coming from his mouth as demons manifested themselves through him.

Rarely is there freedom from opposition to the gospel when it is preached in truth. I remember watching in unbelief as a woman dressed in black stood in front of my crowd as a self-proclaimed prophet to the nation. She had a wooden staff in one hand, and pulled a diamond ring off her finger and threw it at the crowd, saying that it was symbolic that God was divorcing the nation. Then she smashed a bottle on the ground, saying that He would destroy the nation for its iniquity. She claimed that she was alive two thousand years ago, and helped Paul write the Epistles. She also said that as in

the days of Noah, only eight would be saved.
She was one of the eight, and she determined
the other seven. She also maintained that my
spirit visited her in the night. Four-letter filth
words would spill out of her mouth as she
brought God's reproofs to the nation, in perfect King James English of course.

These few incidents, plus a number of others have ingrained in me knowledge of the truth
that we don't wrestle against flesh and blood,
but against hateful spirits, who "work in the
children of disobedience" (Eph. 2:2). Believe
me, your struggle to break out of your comfort
zone is more than a mere fear of man. Jesus
called Satan the father of lies, and the lies come
thick and fast into the ears of those who want
to labor for the gospel. The Bible tells us that
when "the enemy shall come in like a flood, the
Spirit of the Lord shall lift up a standard against
him" (Isa. 59:19). We are seeing the tide of
occultic activity gush upon this world before
our very eyes. Satan is walking about as a roaring lion a little faster than in times past, because his time is short. He is seeking whom he
may devour. At the moment he may devour
many, because many are in his territory.

The subtlety of the spiritual occult realm is
its guise of harmlessness. This was epitomized
in the following letter I received from the manager of a large book publisher:

> Mr. Comfort, it may be of interest to you
> that I specialize in writing books on the
> occult, and you would probably find some

in your local library (occult source-book, other temples, other gods, inner visions, etc., etc). My experience of Christian evaluations of the occult is that they are invariably shallow and misinformed and worse than that, extremely intolerant. How the Hare Krishnas, Mormons, J.W.'s, "The Occult," E.S.P. and T.M. can be classified together, let alone dismissed out of hand, is beyond me. Isn't Christ Himself a mediator who has E.S.P. and healing gifts? P.S. I once had a vision of Christ while on an LSD trip and it was very awe-inspiring. How do you explain that? Was I possessed by the devil?

Years ago, my children attended a school where the principal confided in me that the occult did have a fascination, and that the school now "studied the occult domain each year at Halloween as it studied Christianity at Christmas and Easter," (Halloween is an ancient Druid celebration of death, honoring the god of the dead). He even shared how a ten-year-old had asked him about ectoplasm, which the dictionary says is the "viscous substance exuding from the body of a spiritualistic medium during a trance." My eldest boy came out of class the same day I spoke to the principal and said, "They're still doing it, Dad . . . today we learned about yoga and levitation." I took my kids out of the school that day and put them into a Christian school.

All around us we are seeing fascination for the occult. Psychic hotlines and other demonic activities are being endorsed by celebrities. One magazine carried a real deal for just two dollars: "Yes! Here is the biggest bargain of the decade for the millions of men and women just like you who understand the importance of astrology and luck in your lives."

The advertisement continued to say that this astro-luck package will bring the greatest love, joy and happiness in your life. Along with a special chart came a Maya cross. This little symbol of good fortune was said to bring love and wealth and was referred to as an "ancient talisman." It continued with the words, "obey that impulse . . . order now," and asks the very relevant question, "Will this cross transform your life?"

The word *Maya* comes from Hindu philosophy and means *illusion*. The word illusion, according to the dictionary, means deception.

What's In a Trinket Anyway?

Some years ago, two teen-age girls approached me to see if they could talk to me about the demonic realm. They were both non-Christians and didn't know how to express their concern. I arranged to speak with them the following day. To cut a long story short one of the girls manifested demons on the floor of my office. After she regained consciousness after a time of exorcising prayer, I counselled her to commit her life to Christ and also make a complete break of all occultic practices, which included getting rid of a small trinket which she had around her neck. Two weeks later, I received a phone call from her friend to say that she was still having blackouts. Once again all sorts of demonic manifestations came through this quiet young girl as she lay in a blacked-out state on my office floor.

As she lay there, I noticed she was gripping something around her neck so tightly that all the blood had drained out of her hand. I pried back the fingers of her now white hand to find the trinket I had told her to get rid of. It looked like Tinkerbell, out of *Peter Pan*, and was made of silver. I felt it was probably a goddess of fertility or something similar. I took it from her hand, took it to the other side of my office and hit it with a hammer. She was in a blacked-out state in the far corner of the room. Two of my friends were praying for her; I had my back to her, and yet every time I hit that trinket with the hammer, demons in her screamed. I must have hit it five or six times and as I hit, they screamed; it was like something out of a horror movie.

First Timothy 4:1 warns: "Now the Spirit speaks expressly that, in latter times, some shall depart from the faith, giving heed to seducing spirits, and doctrines of devils."

That is the age in which we are now living. I read an article recently where psychologists related a case of one man having twenty-six different personalities. This newspaper stated that each personality had a complete and separate identity. One psychologist said it was "just like a scene from *The Exorcist*."

I was speaking at a young people's camp
where a seventeen-year-old, nice-looking youth
asked for counsel. His complaint was that he
had an inferiority complex. As I quietly prayed
for him he blacked out, slumped onto the floor,
back-arched, and screamed as demons began to
"rent him sore." Using the authority of the name
of Jesus I commanded the spirits to tell me the
area of stronghold in the young man's life—
"Bitterness!" came the answer.

When he regained consciousness, I counselled him to let go of any bitterness he held
against anybody, justified or unjustified (2 Cor.
2:10-11). I then asked him to tell me what areas
of occult activity he had been involved in. He
listed a number, including ouija boards, LSD,
satanic praise, drinking blood (under the influence of marijuana) and, of course, rock music.
The question arises as to what would cause a
young man to drink blood for kicks. He was
deeply into the ancient rock group AC/DC, and
had been influenced by their album, "You Want
Blood? You've Got It!" Other tracks on their
album were, "Hell ain't such a bad place to be,"
"Rock and Roll Damnation" and "Sin City."

Another group that our young friend was
into was Iron Maiden. They derived their name
from a horrific medieval torture instrument, and
called their third album (a million seller), "The
Number of the Beast." Many other groups
showed obvious links with the demonic world.
The Plasmatics, who took their name from blood
plasma, had tracks "Butcher Baby," "Living

Dead" and "New Hope For The Wretched." Judas Priest sang, "Sin After Sin," while Ozzie Osbourne was well-known for chewing the heads off bats and doves on stage. His albums were aptly named, "Diary of a Madman" and "Paranoid." Cossy Powell, originally known as The Sorcerers, sang their top hit "Dance With The Devil."

The fact that the battle is spiritual, was brought home to me by the following incident. A Christian friend pulled into a fast-food store and heard a local Christian radio station on full volume. He remarked that it was good to hear it, to which the woman behind the counter replied, "I only have it on that station to keep the punk-rockers away. They don't come near this place when that station is playing."

If there is one thing that rock music has in common, it is the spirit of rebellion. The word rebellion is from a root word meaning "bitterness," and means "to be disobedient, to provoke and to rebel." Rebellion in the heart of man is an open invitation for demonic possession. The Scriptures warn that "an evil man seeks only rebellion; therefore, a cruel messenger shall be sent against him" (Prov. 17:11). The word "against" comes from a Hebrew word which is always used in relation to a downward aspect. This was evident in the life of King Saul who was rebuked by Samuel with the words, "Rebellion is as the sin of witchcraft" and followed that downward trend of being tormented by a demonic spirit.

Sin says, "Not Your will, but mine!" Psalm 10:4 tells us that "the wicked, through the pride of his countenance, will not seek after God." It is not that the ungodly cannot find God, it is that he will not. The rebellion of the will is clearly evident in the fall of Lucifer:

> How you are fallen from Heaven, Oh Lucifer, son of the morning! How you are cut down to the ground, you who weakened the nations! For you have said in your heart: I will ascend into Heaven, I will exalt my throne above the stars of God; I will also sit on the mound of the congregation on the farthest sides of the north; I will ascend above the heights of the clouds, I will be like the Most High. (Isa. 14:12-14)

A young punk-rocker once manifested demons at an altar after I had spoken at the church he had started attending. The strongholds in his life were sex, vanity and rock music. I sat the youth down, gave him a drink of water and said, "I want you to pray about your sex life, your musical tastes and do a study on humility." The next evening I received a phone call from him saying that he had taped over all his rock cassettes with Christian music. He also decided to stop frequenting bars (as he had done in the past as a professing Christian), and he was also going to tell his girlfriend that he now loved God, and their immoral sex was over.

He found complete freedom from the demonic realm because he closed the door by an act of his own will. Any Christian who has continued difficulties with demonic possession is still struggling because somewhere there is an open door. The Bible says, "Give no place to the devil." If he "has place" it's because it is being given to him.

Many Christians live in a world of naivety when it comes to the demonic world. We once had a meal with a Christian family, and during the meal the mother got up from the table to turn up the volume on the television so that her son could listen to his favorite hard rock music.

On one of the most popular children's programs on television, I watched in unbelief, as they introduced the program with a group similar to KISS (the SS is shaped like the SS on the Nazi police uniform). The rock group on this program was called "Molech." Molech was the name of the Ammorite idol of the Old Testament, which sat upright with arms outstretched. The arms were heated until they were white hot, then children were placed into its arms as a sacrificial ritual. Drums were constantly played to drown out the screams of the child.

To encourage children into rock music is to place them into the white hot arms of Molech, and the beat and power behind the music will drown out the cries of the child as occultic powers envelop him and take him into the fires of hell.

I received the following letter from a young girl:

> Some time ago, I had a rather frightening experience through listening to rock music

(before I was born again). I've been a Christian since I was about ten years old (I am now fifteen), but I never walked in the light until now.

My girlfriend and her boyfriend were in the dining room while I was in the lounge dancing to some rock music. While I was dancing something made me turn off the light. Suddenly, my body seemed possessed by some kind of spirit (something like the Holy Spirit, but instead of peace, it made me terrified), but I was sort of fascinated. I danced for about one hour not knowing which direction I was facing, moving with the music. When the tape ended I was able to find my way to the switch and turn the light back on. My friends had come into the room and were watching me, I walked over to them and sat down. I couldn't even speak. My friend said to me, "Don't look at me like that, Tracy." I managed to speak by now and asked, "Like what?" She replied: "You've got the devil in you!"

When someone gives themselves over to heavy rock music, they don't get into the spirit . . . it gets into them. The word "wiles" used in Ephesians 6:11, to describe "the wiles of the devil," comes from a Greek word *Methodieas* which is the word from which we derive our English word "method." One of Satan's major methods of snaring this generation has been the international method of music. Maybe you are ignorant of this fact, but ancient rocker David Bowie isn't. He said, "Rock and roll has always been the devil's music—you can't convince me it isn't."

I heard about a young girl who saw a wire hanging from the top of her house. She grabbed the wire with one hand and was fascinated to find that as she moved its raw end across the concrete, sparks began to fly. She then gripped it with both hands and began to wave it back and forth across the concrete with sheer delight, as sparks flashed like sparkling fireworks. Unfortunately, her hand touched a piece of broken wire and a mass of electricity began to flow through her little body. She screamed, "Mommy, Mommy . . . my hands are on fire!" Her mother rushed out of the house, but was flung away with the power when she touched her child. It was then that a passerby ran into the garage, grabbed an axe and cut the wire.

That action saved the little girl's life, but not before she had been severely burned. That story is a graphic illustration of the occult. Satan attracts the mind through fascination, but waits until he has your will—until he has both hands on the wire, before he pours on the heat. Those who escape with severe burns are fortunate compared to the many who don't. The only answer is to sever all connection with the sharp axe of renunciation. Paul speaks of this in 2 Corinthians 4:2: "We have renounced [disowned] the hidden things of dishonesty [Greek shame]."

We also need to realize the authority and the responsibility we have in Jesus Christ. Perhaps we are tempted to look at the Scripture which tells us that when the enemy shall come in like a flood, "the Spirit of the Lord shall lift up a standard against him," and think that it exonerates us from all responsibility. The Spirit of the Lord will lift up a standard against him, but it may be through us. The church is like a man who is searching for his glasses while he is still wearing them. We are looking for God to raise the standard, when God in us is that standard . . . we should be "salt" and "light."

What Should We Then Do?

There is no doubt that the enemy is coming in like a flood, but the question arises as to what we as God's people should do. First, I believe that we should "sanctify the Lord God in our hearts," and our homes. Do we have any idols sitting in our homes in the form of statues, pictures, paperweights, souvenir masks, occultic books, tarot cards, and the like? If you are not sure about a certain item, pray about it and if you have no peace, destroy it. If you have been involved in any of the following practices and have never renounced them, do so from your heart and never open the door to them again. If you have a fascination for the mystics, repent of it, for even the fascination means that the door is slightly open, even if it is only for you to peep through. Desire to look into the mystics is a work of the flesh (Gal. 5:20) which, in the Christian must be reckoned dead. Those who practice such things will not enter the Kingdom of heaven (verse 21), so you don't even want to be tempted.

Have you ever had your fortune told, followed horoscopes, been hypnotized, attended a seance, had involvement in spiritualism, been into hard rock music, "played" with a ouija board, planchette or tarot cards, practiced levitation, chanted mantras, used E.S.P., consulted a medium, sought healing through a spiritualist or color therapy, used good luck charms—rabbit's foot, horseshoes, and others?

I was ministering at a camp when a girl in her late teens approached me, and asked whether or not I thought she should get rid of a rabbit's foot key ring she had been given as a gift. I said that she should pray about it and come to her own decision about destroying it. I had made my mind obvious through the message I had given that morning. She came back the same afternoon and told me that after praying about it she felt the Lord said that it was "O.K. to keep it." That night she manifested demons at the altar.

In another incident, I went to visit a woman who had been having oppressive problems and I was amazed to see a four or five foot carved idol in her living room. It was a gift from her husband, and she felt that as a Christian she should do all that she could to keep peace in the home. I directed her attention to Deuteronomy 7:25-26:

> You shall burn the carved images of their gods with fire; you shall not covet the silver

or gold that is on them, nor take it for
yourselves, lest you be snared by it; for it is
an abomination to the Lord your God. Nor
shall you bring an abomination in your
house, lest you be doomed to destruction
like it; but you shall utterly detest it and
utterly abhor it, for it is an accursed thing.

Her attitude was a little short of what it
should have been, in fact, she had nicknamed
the thing "Charlie." She also manifested demons
at an altar some time later.

Other things on the list which should be
renounced are witchcraft, astroprojection,
occultic children's games such as Dungeons and
Dragons, Masonic Lodge, numerology, wearing
an Ankh cross (similar to the Christian cross
but with a loop at the top), practicing yoga or
practicing martial arts such as karate (some of
these things are harmless to begin with), practicing automatic writing, taking LSD or being
involved with or practicing anything which is of
the mystics. If you have prayed to idols or statues of Jesus or Mary, there also needs to be a
total renunciation (Exod. 20:4-5).

This one is my personal conviction. I am
also convinced that men wearing earrings has
adverse spiritual connotations. They speak of
rebellion and bondage, being very prevalent
among homosexuals, punk-rockers, gypsies and
pirates. Notice in Israel's rebellion of Exodus
chapter 32, that the people "broke off the golden
earrings," which speaks of some sort of bondage to Egypt. A young man told me that he was

about to preach the gospel on a street corner, and God spoke to his heart and said, "You are not preaching My gospel with that thing in your ear." Another Christian was saved out of a rebellious lifestyle, and upon conversion removed the earrings from his ear. Then he was drawn into a group who began murmuring about the pastor. Back in went the earrings. When he understood from Scripture that he was not "murmuring against Moses, but against God," he repented, and immediately took the earrings out again. They were in themselves harmless but were outward indicators of inward rebellion.

I have no right to tell another Christian that he shouldn't wear earrings; that's between him and God, but he should understand that jewelry carries tremendous power in the spiritual domain.

Listen to what a converted witch wrote to me about suicidal thoughts she had:

> Because I still wore the rings that had been given to me on the night of my initiation, I still had contact, and they [those in the witches coven] were able to contact me through my mind.

Those Christians who feel that the international peace movement is a worthy cause to become involved in should take the time to study the origin of the peace symbol. According to the historian, Nestorius, it is an inverted and broken cross. Titus' legions bore it on their shields when they destroyed Jerusalem in A.D.

70 and it then became known as the "broken Jew." It has been used by Arab commandos of the Palestinian Liberation Front. Bolsheviks painted it on the doors of the church buildings they closed in the revolution, and it was branded on the bodies of Jews killed by Communists during the Spanish Civil War.

If you have had any involvement in any of these things listed you need to not only renounce involvement, but you need to destroy the object. Don't sell your rock albums, destroy them, preferably in fire (Acts 19:19, Deut. 7:25).

TWELVE

A Well-trained Housemaid

In the Book of Chronicles, we read of an amazing thing. The Scriptures tell us that Amaziah, king of Judah did that which "was right in the sight of the Lord, but not with a perfect heart" (2 Chron. 25:2). How could someone do something which is "right" in the sight of a perfect God, with an attitude that is less than perfect? The word "perfect" in this case doesn't mean sinless perfection, but comes from a Hebrew word *shalem*, meaning "made ready." It means serving God with a wholeheartedness, with a "Here I am Lord, send me" attitude. I certainly don't want Sue doing that which is right in my sight "but not with a perfect heart." I don't want her to hand me my slippers saying, "Dinner is served, sir," like a well-trained housemaid. No, like every husband, I want my wife to be devoted to me with her whole heart.

Sadly, much of the contemporary church is in the state of doing that which is right, without the perfect heart God desires. We pray, fellow-

ship, tithe, read the Word, yet so few are prepared to break out of their comfort zone, and
take the gospel to every creature, to be "fishers
of men," to preach the Word in season and out
of season . . . to say, "Here I am Lord, send me."

This wholeheartedness is the key to the
power of God being manifest in the church.
The Bible says that "the eyes of the Lord run to
and fro throughout the whole earth, to show
himself strong on behalf of them whose heart is
perfect toward Him" (2 Chron. 16:9). That's the
same word—"perfect." Many Christians are living in defeat because they are not serving God
with a "perfect heart." The Lord is not showing
Himself "strong" on their behalf. We need to
be "willing in the day of (His) power." Part of
our armor listed in Ephesians chapter 6, is to
have our feet shod with the preparation of the
gospel of peace. If we want to effectively resist
the devil, we must totally submit to God. Satan
is terrified of God in the committed Christian.
He knows the power that God gives to the fully
consecrated saint.

Probably the most famous magician and
escape-artist to ever live was Harry Houdini.
Even though he defied death so many times, he
didn't die trying to escape from some death-
defying feat. A young man who had heard about
Houdini's incredibly strong stomach muscles,
approached him backstage and struck him a
blow to the stomach. Unfortunately, Houdini
was caught off-guard and received a ruptured
appendix. Seven days later he died of peritoni-
tis.

Satan trembles at the name of Jesus. He knows that Jesus Christ in us, is infinitely greater than he that is in the world. However, he also knows that the Christian can sometimes be caught backstage and off-guard. That's why there are so many warnings in Scripture about "watching" and being "sober and vigilant, because your adversary the devil walks about as a roaring lion seeking whom he may devour" (1 Pet. 5:8). Each of us needs to have the strong muscle of a holy lifestyle pulled tight to resist the blows of the devil. None of us want to be caught off-guard on the day of wrath. We need to trust in the Lord for our strength, to be "strong in the Lord and in the power of His might."

Fresh Water Surfing

For years I was hooked on surfing. I don't surf now for a number of reasons. There are too many sharks off the coast of southern California seeking that delicious, salt-water delicacy, soft surfer's leg. Besides, if I go for a summer surf and get caught in the freeway traffic, I don't get back until winter. But I will definitely take it up in the millennium when the sharks are friendly, and the water is warm. We will have a thousand years before God does away with the sea, then it's fresh-water surfing for eternity.

Before surfboards became smaller and lighter, we didn't even think of tying them to the leg, as they do nowadays. If you fell off, every instinct within you would tell you to seize the board, because if you didn't, you would have a long swim to the shore to retrieve it. I had no idea how strong this instinct was, until I tried water-skiing.

I took off after the boat, and things were fine for about ten seconds. Suddenly, I fell and found myself being dragged under the water for about thirty feet. My impulse was to hang onto the rope even though I was under the water. Dummy! I ended up with a head full of salt water.

When we come to Christ, our sinful nature doesn't want to let go of pet sins. Habitual sin is ingrained in our nature, but if we have any sense, we will let go of the rope, because sin will do nothing but drag us down.

A twenty-year-old man was on a snowmobile in Colfax, Iowa, in the late seventies. He was having a ball, racing around on the glistening white snow. He swung the machine around and sped at about thirty miles an hour between two wooden posts. That was the last thing he did. A thin, almost invisible wire between the posts decapitated him.

Satan will let you have a ball. He will let you race around and enjoy the pleasures of sin for a season. You are in his territory, so you therefore give him permission to devour you. The devil walks around as a roaring lion seeking whom he *may* devour. His will is only to "kill, steal and destroy," and somewhere he has a wire strung at just the right height for your neck. All he needs is a little cooperation. He wants you to put your foot on the accelerator and get up a little speed.

How to Succeed as a Thief

A popular magazine once ran an article by an ex-cat burglar. He didn't steal cats, he preyed on the homes of those of us who are ignorant of his ways. Most of us, because of a lack of knowledge, virtually put a sign up saying, "Thieves, I'm outta town, so come in and steal what you want."

This is how we do it. We have unlit rear entrances which are enshrouded by trees and hedges. They act as a magnet for the burglar. The ex-thief said that a loud airconditioner was an open invitation. If people could sleep through its noise, they weren't going to hear him breaking into their home.

He would even masquerade as a newspaper-subscription salesman, knocking on doors, ready to do a phony sales pitch if anyone answered. Then he would leave a card on the door handle, and if no one answered and it was still there the next day, it was a sure sign that the family was away.

A name on the mailbox gives the burglar all the information he needs to find your phone number and call to see if you are home. Even alarms don't guarantee security. Often people put the alarm sticker on the front of their house to scare away would-be burglars. All the burglars do is write a letter to the company and say they are wanting to purchase an alarm system.

They then study the literature to become familiar with it so they can easily disarm it. Exterior alarms can be filled with shaving cream to silence them, while most locks can be simply picked. Windows can be silently broken, by putting a paper covered with Vaseline on it, so that when they break, they do so silently.

He says that most people lay their house out like a candy store. They place their jewelry, wallet or purse in the bedroom or by the kitchen sink, and if he needs a car, the keys are on the end of the counter. The man's best advice to stop burglars: "Get two dogs. Make sure they bark." He said that even a house guarded by a Chihuahua is well protected, because people wake up when the dog barks. He advises that if you hear a burglar in the house not to confront him. If he has a gun, he will probably shoot you and even all the family, rather than go to prison. His advice, and the advice of the law, is to call the police.

Satan knows what he is doing. He is an expert in his field. He sees many signs that tell him he is safe to make entrance. A dusty Bible is an open invitation. Lack of the light of good understanding is another open attraction. He wants us to be in the dark—to be "ignorant of his devices." He wants a sleeping Christian, someone not watching and praying, as Jesus told us to.

Don't confront the devil, call upon God for backup. If you have a problem with lust, realize that it is a weapon of darkness that will be the death of you. Call upon the Lord. Tell Him to disarm the devil. Tell Him that you don't want that creep creeping around in your property. He only comes in the dark, and you need to walk in the light to keep him away. Have the guard dog of a good conscience, and listen when he barks. He is there to protect you.

Dogmatic Resistance

Even before I was converted, I stumbled upon a major scriptural principle. I was riding my motorbike home from work, when a rather large, vicious German shepherd rushed out of a driveway and began to snap at my back tire. As I was about to pour the power on (it was a Honda 50) and leave the animal in the dust, I had a thought: "Wait a minute! Greater is that which I am sitting on than that which is chasing me!" I then stopped the bike, much to the bewilderment of the dog, turned it around and chased that animal up the street.

If Satan is chasing you, slam on the brakes and say, "Greater is He that is in me, than he that is in the world," (1 John 4:4) then submit afresh to God, resist the devil, and he will flee from you. You have God's promise on that (James 4:7).

I once showed up in the local square to find that one of my preaching buddies was being hampered by peace protesters. They were holding a rally on the other side of the square and had come across to ask him to stop preaching. Their argument was that "we were all on the same side, both standing for peace." I gently told them that we preach peace with God while the peace movement preached peace without God.

I then told my friend to keep preaching. That upset the peace people, to a point where they persistently pushed, pulled and poked at the preacher. When they stopped him, I felt something erupt within me and immediately began preaching about twenty feet away. They ran towards me to stop me from speaking, and when they stopped me, my friend Wally burst into flames, and so it went on until they gave up.

If you have never felt the wind of persecution blow upon the fire of the Holy Spirit within you, you are missing out on something amazing. You don't know what power dwells in you until that fan fuels the flame and sparks a boldness in your spirit. We have tapped into the supernatural realm. The Bible tells us, "that when Saul made havoc of the church," the disciples were scattered abroad and went everywhere preaching the Word (Acts 8:3-4). Saul merely stirred the winds of persecution. When Paul was placed in prison, he wrote that "many of the brethren in the Lord, waxing confidence in my bonds, are much more bold to speak the Word without fear" (Phil. 1:14). Others took up the mantle of Saul of Tarsus, and now persecution against Paul stirred the fire in his brethren. He went on to write "in nothing [be] terrified by your adversaries."

Sue and I were once trying to prize resistant nuts from their shells. They would crack open, but were very difficult to get out from the inside of their casings. Suddenly, a bright idea struck me. I put one in the microwave oven for ten seconds. Then, when I cracked the nut, no longer did it cling to the shell, but came out without the slightest resistance.

If there is one thing that will bring the timid Christian out of his shell it is the heat of persecution. That's all that happened when God allowed Saul to put the early church in the heat of the microwave. Persecution put the fear of God in the hearts of those who were exercised by it. The Puritan author, William Gurnall, the author of *The Christian in Complete Armour* of which Spurgeon said, "Gurnall's work is peerless and priceless," said: "We fear men so much, because we fear God so little. One fear causes another. When man's terror scares you, turn your thoughts to the wrath of God."

Trials also can have the effect of bringing us to our knees and seeking God's will rather than our own. In South Korea, a baseball team called the Dolphins began a training program with a difference. They would climb a high mountain, remove their shirts and stand bare-chested in the freezing wind. Then they would dig holes in the ice, and subject their bodies to freezing water. They said that it made the team hardy and also promoted team unity. They went from being a laughing stock, to the top of the league. Now all the other teams have imitated their training program.

As much as we don't like the thought, bless-
ings tend to take our eyes off God, and trials
put them back on God. Icy tribulation builds
strength of character within the Christian, and
the cold winds of persecution purify the church
bringing a sense of unity of purpose. However,
if we chasten ourselves, we need not be chas-
tened. We must focus our hearts on God now.
Without a genuine move of His Spirit in the
near future, an entire generation will destroy
itself. The government took the Ten Commandments off the walls of the schools, and prayer
from the classroom, and it is reaping a whirl-
wind of destruction. When there is no wall of
absolute authority, anarchy comes in like a flood.
When a generation has no fear of God before
their eyes, then the laws which forbid murder
have no influence. On any given day in the
United States, an estimated one hundred thousand guns and knives are smuggled into schools.

How on earth do we move the hand of the
God of heaven? The answer is, and has always
been twofold. We must first get on our knees
and beseech God to save this generation, then
ask Him to use us to take the means of salvation to the unsaved. He has chosen the foolishness of preaching to save the lost. He has entrusted us with the word of reconciliation, and
it is therefore up to us to break free from that
which binds us, and obey His great commission
to preach the gospel to every creature.

Three men who broke out of their comfort

zone, were Shadrach, Meshach and Abed-Nego.
The king told them to bow down to his idol, but
rather than sin against God, they refused. They
knew the Law:

> I am the Lord your God who brought you
> out of Egypt, out of the house of bondage.
> You shall have no other gods before Me.
> You shall not make for yourself a graven
> image, or any likeness of anything that is in
> heaven above, or that is in the earth be-
> neath, or that is in the water under the
> earth; you shall not bow down to them nor
> serve them. For I am a jealous God, visiting
> the iniquity of the fathers on the children
> to the third and fourth generations of those
> that hate Me, but showing mercy to thou-
> sands, to those who love me and keep My
> Commandments. (Exod. 20:1-6)

The three godly men loved God and therefore kept His commandments. Their choice was
to compromise and keep in good with the king,
or obey God and be cast into the fiery furnace.
These men knew what was acceptable. Like
David when he faced Goliath, they didn't need
to seek the mind of the Lord in this matter,
because the Law had already given them knowledge of right from wrong. Look at what they
said to the king when he threatened them with
such a terrible death:

> O Nebuchadnezzar, we have no need to
> answer you in this matter. If that is the
> case, our God whom we serve is able to
> deliver us from the burning fiery furnace,

and He will deliver us from your hand, O
king. But if not, let it be known to you O
king, that we do not serve your gods, nor
will we worship the gold image which you
have set up. (Dan. 3:16-18)

The Christian will not bow down to the
golden image of mammon, with its promise of
gratification, security and comfort. Even if the
devil threatens to heat up the furnace of persecution and tribulation seven times, he will not
bow down. He looks to the Word of God as his
authority "denying ungodliness and worldly
lusts." He is a disciple of Christ and therefore
thanks God that he has been counted worthy to
suffer for the name of the Savior. He is as Moses
who broke free from the comfort zone of Egypt,
"choosing rather to suffer affliction with the
people of God than to enjoy the passing pleasures of sin."

How can you extend yourself within your
Christian walk? In the natural realm, we cause
muscle growth through resistance. If you want
to grow physically, get into a swimming pool
and hold a five gallon container filled with water
at head level. To stay afloat, you will have to
kick for dear life. The key in this exercise is to
have the lid off the container, face it down and
let the water drain out as you kick. A great
consolation is that you know that as time passes,
as you tire, the weight is going to get lighter,
and that knowledge will spur you on.

As you step into the waters of personal evangelism, the weight of apprehension may seem

unbearable, but as you pour yourself out for the gospel, you will have the knowledge that God will relieve you of the weight. Each time you exercise yourself in this, you will strengthen yourself spiritually.

The Land of Uz

A man once challenged Charles Spurgeon to give him one Scripture against infant baptism, and he would give one to Spurgeon which supported the practice. The man said, "Suffer the little children to come to Me." Spurgeon looked at the man and said, "There was a man in the land of Uz, whose name was Job" (Job 1:1). The man protested, "That verse has nothing to do with infant baptism!" To which the wise preacher answered, "And neither has yours."

There are certain doctrines that are built upon very feeble foundations. There are one or two Scriptures to support a particular interpretation, but when it comes to our responsibility to reach out to the lost, there stands before us a great concrete infrastructure to build upon. The reason Jesus came to this earth was to save sinners from eternal justice. The solid steel-enforced framework of many foundational Scriptures support our evangelical obligations.

When you break out from your securities and seek the lost, even if it's dropping tracts on seats at an airport, you are in the front line of the battle. We need each other, so link arms through the Spirit with your brethren through-

out the world. Determine to take advantage of
every minute of the day to reach this world
while there is still time. When you are not witnessing, be in an attitude of prayer, praying
that God will make you effective, that He will
give you wisdom and the motivation to break
free from the fears that hinder you from reaching out to the world. Keep yourself always ready
to share your faith, so that you will never be
caught off-guard.

Years ago, someone told me that a new
convert was about to have an abortion. When I
enquired as to when, I found out that the operation was about to take place that very afternoon at two o'clock. It was already one o'clock
as I sped into the hospital parking lot. I ran
through the hospital and up to the second floor,
praying that God would give me the words, the
wisdom, and the discretion to stop this young
woman taking the life of her child.

When I entered her room I found her sitting on the bed. She had already had her pre-
operative medication. I looked into her eyes
and said the only thing that came to mind—
"Please . . . don't do this thing." She smiled
warmly and said, "It's alright. I'm not going
through with it. I have just finished praying,
'God, if you don't want me to have an abortion,
make Ray Comfort come in and speak to me.'"

I left the hospital walking on air. God had
just used me in the saving of a human life. He
didn't use my words or my wisdom, he just
used me. It gave me a warm feeling to know

that God would take the time to do such a thing. Yet, I never really realized what God had used me for until about two years later at a church picnic, when I saw a cute little girl playing by herself on the grass. As I bent down to her, I realized that this was the same child that was going to be aborted. It was then, as I looked into her little face, that I fully understood what God had used me for that day.

The most zealous of us hasn't any real depth of understanding as to what God is using us for when we are involved in evangelism. We have a measure of appreciation that God is using us to plant the seed of the gospel in the hearts of those who are in the shadow of death. However, I don't think it will fully dawn upon us as to what God is using us for, until the day when a vast sea of billions of humanity stand before the judgment throne of Almighty God. The Great Shepherd stands from the great white throne, and separates the sheep from the goats. Suddenly, we see someone to whom we passed a tract or someone we witnessed to, separated to everlasting life!

Perhaps then, and only then, will we fully comprehend what God is using us for, but it is my prayer that He will give us understanding now as to the privilege we have, in being entrusted with the gospel of everlasting life.

Hive of Activity

Pray that God would raise up more laborers, because there are so few. Some time ago, I finished speaking at a church in Minneapolis, when the pastor of evangelism took hold of the microphone. He was an ex-cop, and his voice cracked with emotion as he spoke of an accident victim he once held in his arms. The critically injured man thrashed back and forth for a moment, sighed deeply, then passed into eternity. The pastor's voice was filled with emotion, because his own church had over a thousand members, and only five attended his evangelism class. It was obvious that the church's hive of activity was in the comfort zone of everything but evangelism. He pleaded, saying, "What's wrong with you? Don't you care that people in our city are going to Hell? I can teach you to rid yourself of fear." His was no proud boast. The prison doors of fear can be opened with very simple keys—a knowledge of God's will, ordered priorities, love that is not passive, gratitude for the cross, and the use of the Law before grace.

On a warm spring day in New York, a fire broke out in a high-rise building. When firemen arrived, they saw a man on a ledge on the twelfth floor. Smoke billowed out from the building, blinding the terrified man and forcing him to the very edge. Death seemed to lick its lips.

Quickly, a fireman was lowered from above by a rope, and thankfully rescued him before he was forced to jump to his death. The delivered man said that it was a miracle that he was saved. He said that he was blind, but heard the voice of his rescuer, and from there clung to him for dear life.

How perfectly that sums up our salvation. We had climbed the stairs of the high-rise of sin, and found that the law of sin and death forced us onto the ledge of futility. We stood blind, fearful, helpless and hopeless . . . until we heard the voice of our Savior. We heard the joyful sound of the voice of the Son of God, as He reached out His holy hand and snatched us from death's dark door. But there are still others on the ledge going through the terror we once experienced. We cannot rest until we direct them into the hands of Jesus.

I thank God that He saved me while I was young, while I still have energy to reach out to the lost. I pray that God will make me to know the number of my days that I might "apply my heart to wisdom," and it's the epitome of wisdom to spend every ounce of energy and every moment of every day seeking the salvation of souls. There is no higher calling.

In closing, I would like to pray for you, but before I do, let me remind you of two things. The first is that every time you venture out of your comfort zone you are going to battle fear. When you size someone up before you approach them to give them a tract or witness to them you will hear a voice say, "Are you kidding! Look at the guy . . . *and you think you are going to give him a tract?* He's an obvious Christian-hater if ever I saw one. Look at his Christian-hating jaw and his Christian-strangling hands. He's praying for some self-righteous fanatic to

try and ram religion down his throat, and as
soon as you open your mouth, he's going to rip
your ears off. He will humiliate you. No, you
shouldn't do this. Don't be a fool, go back to
your comfort zone." But don't take any notice—
he's a liar from the beginning. You will almost
always find that the grizzly bear waiting to kill
you is actually a teddy bear wanting to cuddle
you. If you speak the truth in love, he will re-
spond to that love.

I remember once going down to the local
municipal courts and waiting to witness to anyone who would listen. There was hardly a soul
in sight so I said, "Lord, I will wait here for five
minutes, and if no one comes I will go home."

Three minutes later, I watched a couple in
their twenties sit down about fifty feet from me.
I said, "No Lord, I want people to be by themselves. People are more open when they are
alone." I was about to go back to the Comfort
Zone (we have a sign on our house saying The
Comfort Zone), but I felt so guilty, I reluctantly
walked across, sat down beside them and gave
them both an I.Q. tract. They said that they had
Charismatic Christian backgrounds, but I felt
that they weren't right with God so I said to the
young lady, "Do you think you have obeyed the
Ten Commandments?" When I asked her if she
had ever told a lie, she said she had. I asked,
"What does that make you?" She said, "A sinner." When I said, "a *liar*," her mouth dropped
open in shock. It was obvious that she had never
thought of herself as a liar, but I told her that

is how God sees her and when I reasoned with her about it she nodded in agreement. She also admitted that she had broken the other commandments and agreed that if she died in the state she was in she would go to hell.

Then I turned to both of them and said, "No fornicator will enter heaven. If you have sex before marriage that is breaking the Seventh Commandment also. God sees everything you do; He even knows how many hairs are on your head!"

The young man looked at me in unbelief and said, "That's weird. *I was just reading that this morning!*" He then brought out a pocket book of God's promises and said that he was in bed with his girlfriend reading about the fact that no fornicator would enter God's Kingdom and that He knew how many hairs were on his head. *He was reading Scriptures until 4:00 A.M. and was so stirred that his girlfriend thought he was on drugs.*

I told them that they needed to repent, put their faith in Jesus and live according to His Word. That meant they must stop having sex and get married, if they loved each other, *then* they could enjoy the pleasures of sex. I said, "Imagine if you had twenty dollars that you were going to give to your son as a surprise, but an hour before you were to give it to him he stole it out of your wallet. That's what you have done with the gift of sex." They both nodded, and we prayed together. Thank God I didn't go back home. The devil's a liar and if the fears come thick and strong, you can be sure God wants to use you for His purposes.

The second thing I want to remind you of is in the form of a question. Imagine if I said to you that I was working for the UCLA Medical Institute, and that our scientists, due to recent changes in the law, can now pay big money for human eyes. Not only could your eye give sight to a blind person, but you would walk away with one million dollars in cool, tax-free cash. What's more, the operation would be totally painless, take less than one hour, and the new eye would look as good as the authentic one. You will look the same; but you won't *look* the same . . . one eye will be blind. *Would you sell me one of your eyes for a million dollars?*

Perhaps you would sell just one eye for a million dollars. *How about selling both for fifteen million?* Think for a moment what you would do with all that money—you could see the world. Not quite. You could sit at home in the blackness of blindness and count it. I'm sure no one in their right mind would consider selling his or her eyesight for *fifty* million dollars!

Perhaps you have never given it any deep thought, but your eyes are priceless, and yet they are merely the windows of the soul—the "life" that peers through the shutters of your eyes. If your eyes are without price, *what must your life be worth?* In fact, Jesus said that your life is so valuable, you are to actually *despise* your eyes in comparison to the worth of your soul. He said that if your right eye causes you to sin, you are to pluck it out and cast it from you, for it would be better to go to heaven without an eye than to go to hell, where the "worm never dies and the fire is never quenched." He said that the combined riches of this entire world are not worth losing your soul—"What shall it profit a man if he gains the whole world and loses his soul?"

Of all the things you should prioritize in your life, it's your eternal salvation. The most important thing in your life is not your health, your marriage, your vocation . . . it is the salvation of your soul. These things are merely temporal, your salvation is eternal, so don't let *anything* hinder your obedience to God. Despise sin and the world. Cast out ungodly thoughts. Let love for God and man be your governing dictate, and pray . . . pray that God would use you, that He would make you even more effective in your labors for Him, that He would help you to break out of your comfort zone and do exploits for Him:

> Father, in Jesus' name, I pray for this dear reader who so desires to reach those in darkness with Your message of forgiveness. Your Word says that if we delight ourselves in You, You will give us our heart's desire. Oh God, we desire above all things that this world be reached with Your love and forgiveness. Grant us that wisdom, that love, that heavenly anointing we so need to be effective. Cause us to be prayer-warriors, men and women of faith, power and bold-

ness. Help us to lay aside those hindering weights and besetting sins, to live in victory and joy unspeakable, so that others might see You in us. Help us to "run on water" with the message, to use Your Law effectively, to work out our salvation with "fear and trembling," and to work for the world's salvation. Lay "necessity" upon us. Banish the fear of man from our hearts. May we meditate upon Your Law day and night, that we might bear lasting fruit and have "good success" in our labors for You. We ask this for the glory of Your precious Name, and for the extension of Your everlasting Kingdom . . . in Jesus' name, AMEN!

We welcome comments from our readers. Feel free to write to us at the following address:

Editorial Department
Huntington House Publishers
P.O. Box 53788
Lafayette, LA 70505

================

More Good Books from Huntington House

Revival:
Its Principles and Personalities
by Winkie Pratney

Are you disturbed by the apathy and despondency of people today? Do you wonder what the future holds for this immoral world? In an age in which values are questioned, families are falling apart, and quality is being replaced by quantity, there is an ever-growing need for a revival of the morals and beliefs of a more stable time. This book is a guide to revival, focusing on past revivals—their personalities and principles—in order to stir all people to seek and expect future revivals.

ISBN 1-56384-058-8 $10.99

Hungry for God
Are the Poor Really Unspiritual?
by Larry E. Myers

Inspired by the conviction that the blood of Jesus is the great equalizer, Larry Myers set out to bring much-needed hope and relief to the desperately poor of Mexico. You will be deeply moved by these people, who have so little yet worship their Lord and Savior, even in the midst of their need. You will be inspired by Larry Myers's determination to bring not only medical supplies and food, but light and life to those hungry for God.

ISBN 1056384-075-8 $9.99

The Extermination of Christianity
by Paul Schenck with Robert L. Schenck

If you are a Christian, you might be shocked to discover that: Popular music, television, and motion pictures are consistently depicting you as a stooge, a hypocrite, a charlatan, a racist, an anti-Semite, or a con artist; you could be expelled from a public high school for giving Christian literature to a classmate; and you could be arrested and jailed for praying on school grounds. This book is a catalogue of anti-Christian propaganda—a record of persecution before it happens!

ISBN 1-56384-051-0 $9.99

Combat Ready
How to Fight the Culture War
by Lynn Stanley

The culture war between traditional values and secular humanism is escalating. At stake are our children. The schools, the liberal media, and even the government, through Outcome Based Education, are indoctrinating our children with moral relativism, instead of moral principles. *Combat Ready* not only discloses the extent to which our society has been influenced by this "anything goes" mentality. It offers sound advice about how parents can protect their children and restore our culture to its biblical foundation.

ISBN 1-56384-074-X $9.99

High on Adventure
Stories of Good, Clean,
Spine-tingling Fun
by Stephen Arrington

From meeting a seventeen-and-a-half-foot great white shark face to face, to diving from an airplane toward the earth's surface at 140 M.P.H., to exploring a sunken battle cruiser from World War II in the dark depths of the South Pacific Ocean, author and adventurer Stephen Arrington retells many exciting tales from his life as a navy frogman and chief diver for the Cousteau Society. Each story is laced with Arrington's Christian belief and outlook that life is an adventure waiting to be had.

ISBN 1-56384-082-0 $7.99

Can Families Survive in
Pagan America?
by Samuel Dresner

Drug addiction, child abuse, divorce, and the welfare state have dealt terrible, pounding blows to the family structure. At the same time, robbery, homicide, and violent assaults have increased at terrifying rates. But, according to the author, we can restore order to our country and our lives. Using the tenets of Jewish family life and faith, Dr. Dresner calls on Americans from every religion and walk of life to band together and make strong, traditional families a personal and national priority again—before it's too late.

ISBN Trade Paper: 1-56384-080-4 $15.99
Hardcover: 1-56384-086-3 $31.99

ORDER THESE HUNTINGTON HOUSE BOOKS !

- America Betrayed—Marlin Maddoux...................................7.99
- The Assault—Dale A. Berryhill......................................9.99
- Beyond Political Correctness—David Thibodaux........................9.99
- The Best of HUMAN EVENTS—Edited by James C. Roberts.................34.95
- Can Families Survive in Pagan America?—Samuel Dresner......15.99/31.99 HB
- Circle of Death—Richmond Odom......................................9.99
- Combat Ready—Lynn Stanley..9.99
- Conservative, American & Jewish—Jacob Neusner......................9.99
- The Dark Side of Freemasonry—Ed Decker.............................9.99
- The Demonic Roots of Globalism—Gary Kah............................9.99
- Don't Touch That Dial—Barbara Hattemer & Robert Showers.....9.99/19.99 HB
- En Route to Global Occupation—Gary Kah.............................9.99
- *Exposing the AIDS Scandal—Dr. Paul Cameron...................7.99/2.99
- Freud's War with God—Jack Wright, Jr...............................7.99
- Goddess Earth—Samantha Smith.......................................9.99
- Gays & Guns—John Eidsmoe.......................................7.99/14.99 HB
- Health Begins in Him—Terry Dorian.................................9.99
- Heresy Hunters—Jim Spencer...8.99
- Hidden Dangers of the Rainbow—Constance Cumbey....................9.99
- High-Voltage Christianity—Michael Brown............................9.99
- Homeless in America—Jeremy Reynalds...............................9.99
- How to Homeschool (Yes, You!)—Julia Toto...........................4.99
- Hungry for God—Larry E. Myers......................................9.99
- I Shot an Elephant in My Pajamas—Morrie Ryskind w/ John Roberts......12.99
- *Inside the New Age Nightmare—Randall Baer.....................9.99/2.99
- A Jewish Conservative Looks at Pagan America—Don Feder.....9.99/19.99 HB
- Journey into Darkness—Stephen Arrington............................9.99
- Kinsey, Sex and Fraud—Dr. Judith A. Reisman & Edward Eichel.........11.99
- The Liberal Contradiction—Dale A. Berryhill........................9.99
- Legalized Gambling—John Eidsmoe....................................7.99
- Loyal Opposition—John Eidsmoe......................................8.99
- The Media Hates Conservatives—Dale A. Berryhill...........9.99/19.99 HB
- New Gods for a New Age—Richmond Odom...............................9.99
- One Man, One Woman, One Lifetime—Rabbi Reuven Bulka................7.99
- Out of Control—Brenda Scott...................................9.99/19.99 HB
- Outcome-Based Education—Peg Luksik & Pamela Hoffecker..............9.99
- The Parched Soul of America—Leslie Kay Hedger w/ Dave Reagan.......10.99
- Please Tell Me—Tom McKenney..9.99
- Political Correctness—David Thibodaux..............................9.99
- Resurrecting the Third Reich—Richard Terrell.......................9.99
- Revival: Its Principles and Personalities—Winkie Pratney...........10.99
- Trojan Horse—Brenda Scott & Samantha Smith.........................9.99
- The Walking Wounded—Jeremy Reynalds................................9.99

*Available in Salt Series

Available at bookstores everywhere or order direct from:
Huntington House Publishers • P.O. Box 53788 • Lafayette, LA 70505
Send check/money order. For faster service use VISA/MASTERCARD.
Call toll-free 1-800-749-4009.
Add: Freight and handling, $3.50 for the first book ordered, and $.50 for
each additional book up to 5 books.